ACCELERATING OUT of the GREAT RECESSION

How to Win in a Slow-Growth Economy

David Rhodes and Daniel Stelter
THE BOSTON CONSULTING GROUP

New York Chicago San Francisco Lisbon
London Madrid Mexico City
Milan New Delhi San Juan Seoul
Singapore Sydney Toronto

The **McGraw·Hill** Companies

1 2 3 4 5 6 7 8 9 0   DOC/DOC   1 0 9 8 7 6 5 4 3 2 1 0

ISBN: 978-0-07-171814-1
MHID: 0-07-171814-1

McGraw-Hill books are available at special quantity discounts to use as premiums and sales promotions, or for use in corporate training programs. To contact a representative please e-mail us at bulksales@mcgraw-hill.com.

For our wives, Alex and Brunhild

CONTENTS

PART TWO

CHAPTER 3

CHAPTER 4

CHAPTER 5

ACKNOWLEDGMENTS

In the year following the collapse of Lehman Brothers, we wrote a series of papers entitled *Collateral Damage*, laying out our view of the developing economic crisis, the emerging "new realities," and the actions companies needed to take to prosper in a damaged economy. Some of the ideas in those papers, together with some of the research, helped to underpin this book.

A number of colleagues at The Boston Consulting Group (BCG) helped us to develop that thinking, and we wish to acknowledge their contribution to our work. In no particular order, they are Shubh Saumya, André Kronimus, Sylvain Duranton, Andrew Dyer, Philip Evans, Mike Deimler, Grant Freeland, Jean-Manuel Izaret, Andy Maguire, David Michael, Takashi Mitachi, Alexander Roos, Jeff Gell, Janmejaya Sinha, Bernd Waltermann, Chuck Scullion, Rainer Strack, Stépan Breedveld, Rune Jacobsen, Frank Plaschke, Gerry Hansell, Lars-Uwe Luther, Jeff Kotzen, Eric Olsen, Jens Kengelbach, Mathias Schatt, and Catherine Roche.

There is a small group of people who came with us on pretty much the whole journey. They dug out obscure data from long ago, they helped to research the archives, they were our eyes and ears on the developing economic story, and they helped to make the experience a most rewarding one for us. We want to thank Nimisha Jain, Jendrik Odewald, Katrin van Dyken, Jim Minifie, Renato Matiolli, William Gore-Randall, Carolin Eistert, Kyrill Radev, Daniel Schneider, and Hiroki Inada for their wholehearted efforts.

In addition, BCG's editor-in-chief, Simon Targett, provided wise counsel throughout the challenging process of writing this book, while John Butman contributed his experience in the art of writing business books. Mary Glenn, our publisher at McGraw-Hill, encouraged us to develop our work as a book, and Knox Huston, our editor at McGraw-Hill, was both constructive and responsive—and we thank them for this. We would also like to thank Todd Shuster, our literary agent, of Zachary Shuster Harmsworth, and Eric Gregoire of BCG, who helped our promotional efforts.

But there are two people who deserve special mention: Alex Dewar and Namrata Harishanker not only helped with all the research and the development of our ideas but also made enormous contributions to the writing of the book itself. We thank them for their hard work, for their unceasing good humor in the face of our unreasonable requests, and—most of all—for the quality of their contribution. Any shortcomings are ours alone.

INTRODUCTION

In the Aftermath of the Great Recession

It was not at all what the experts predicted. Most of them did not foresee that an economic powerhouse could suffer so much damage in such a short period of time. They did not expect the fast-growing gross domestic product (GDP) to go so spectacularly into reverse, the real estate bubble to burst as violently as it did, and industrial production and capacity utilization to fall so steeply. Nor did they expect the stock market to plunge so dramatically from its all-time high—although it would recover some ground subsequently.

No, the Japanese (and Western) economists and analysts of 1991 predicted none of these developments. They expected that the 4 percent compound annual growth rate in real GDP that Japan had enjoyed for a decade would continue unabated. They expected that incomes, property values, industrial production, profits, and share prices would continue to rise.

But, as we know, Japan entered what is today called the Lost Decade. Between 1991 and 2001, its compound annual growth barely crept above 1 percent. The Japanese government dithered while the economy faltered. And, although there were a few quarters when things seemed to be improving, the Lost Decade actually extended considerably beyond 10 years.

Are we saying that the United States of 2009 is comparable with the Japan of 1991? Not exactly. The economies of the two countries are very different, as are the cultures and (critically) the demographics of the two populations. Also, the U.S. government responded faster and more aggressively to the financial crisis than Japan's government did nearly 20 years ago.

But the real issue is not what *has* happened, but what happens *next*. Will the United States experience its own version of Japan's Lost Decade? Many experts seem to assume that history, albeit displaced by a few time zones, will not repeat itself. But what if the present recovery were to resemble the experience in Japan?

In a survey of top executives we conducted in the fall of 2009, nearly half the respondents said that they expected postrecession growth to be anemic for an extended period. Thus, given the high risk that history *may* be repeating itself, companies should be acting as if it *could*. They should be figuring out—now—how to thrive in what many believe will be an economy operating in a damaged state for years to come. They should be acclimatizing to what has become known as the "new normal."

There are, of course, many voices arguing that nothing has really changed, that things will soon return to the "old normal." As evidence that not so much is different, they point to the apparent recovery in the banking system and some green shoots of global growth as 2009 drew to a close. But, as we describe in the first two chapters of this book, we believe that such complacency is ill-founded.

This is not a book about economics in general or any economy in particular. This is a book about strategy and management. We are interested in the fallout of what is being called the Great Recession because the nature of the recovery forms the backdrop against which management must make the strategic and operating decisions that shape their companies.

And an awful lot hangs on whether a business leader foresees a fast- or a slow-growing world. Even if business leaders do not subscribe to the view that economic growth will be slow, we still believe that they cannot go wrong by following the line of logic set out by the philosopher Blaise Pascal in his work *Pensées*. He was not sure whether God existed, but—in what has become known as "Pascal's wager"—he argued that it is most prudent to act as if there is, in fact, a deity. The consequences of living a life of a nonbeliever—only to discover, at the moment of death, that such a path was wrong—are too dire to risk. When it comes to business management, the analogous quandary is the question of economic growth.

To set a context for our thoughts on strategy and management, we need to come clean on our assumptions about growth—which are firmly rooted in our view on the nature of the recovery in the United States. U.S. consumers drove the global boom, and they will determine—through their changing habits and behaviors—many of the "new realities" that we believe will shape the global economy (more on this in Chapter 2).

It is not only the fact that U.S. consumers generate a very large share of global GDP—on the order of 18.8 percent—that makes their contribution so important; it is also that there is no obvious short-term replacement for this mainstay of the global economy. There may be four times as many consumers in China as there are in the United States (and Chinese households also tend to have stronger balance sheets), but Chinese consumers simply do not have the wealth or spending power of the U.S.

consumer, even in tough economic times. In 2008, total private consumption in China was equivalent to just 15 percent of total U.S. consumer spending, or 2.9 percent on a per capita basis. Thus, a 32 percent increase in private consumption in China would be needed to offset just a 5 percent reduction in U.S. consumer spending.

This is not going to happen.

China is not a strong enough economic engine to pull the whole world back into a period of high growth, even though it is the world's fourth-largest economy and accounted for nearly a quarter of total global growth in 2008. There are just too many developed countries (including the most important one in the world) suffering from the effects of a severely damaged economy for China to pull off a kind of indirect global bailout.

So we do not subscribe yet to the theory of decoupling. We remain concerned about the United States because it *is* still the main economic player on the global stage. Over the next few years, the Indian and Chinese economies may well perform spectacularly. So in time, it may indeed no longer be axiomatic that when the United States sneezes, the world catches a cold. But for a while yet, at least, any economic ills of the United States still matter to the wider world.

Put plainly: We believe that much of the world is now entering a period of prolonged slower growth, as we will discuss in the coming chapters. This is of great significance to business leaders and executives—for at least five reasons:

1. *It increases the competitive intensity of business.* In order to grow, companies will have to gain market share. The management teams and strategies of all companies—

especially poorly run ones—will be placed under enormous stress. This will force the reshaping of the competitive landscape in many industries, as well as the redefining of fundamental business dynamics.

2. *It prompts governments to become more activist.* We expect to see an increase in protectionism—embracing trade, employment, reindustrialization, and finance. There will be greater regulation, and some governments will further tinker with fiscal and monetary policy, whereas others will take on greater ownership of private enterprises.

3. *It forces a change in the nature of consumption.* Consumers in emerging markets may well increase their spending, but not by enough to offset the weak growth in consumption in the United States and Western Europe, where consumers will save more in the face of greater job insecurity and reduced retirement provisions.

4. *It triggers a process of deleveraging.* This occurs as individuals and companies (and eventually governments), weighed down by huge and unsustainable levels of debt, recognize that it is payback time. This will act as a further drag on global economic growth.

5. *It sparks an acceleration in industry restructuring.* Tough economic times tend to expose structural weaknesses—just look at the U.S. auto industry. Poorly grounded business models and excess capacity, among other problems, will force companies—especially those in mature industries—to adjust to or exit the market.

Yet, even within a low-growth economy, and despite all this change and restructuring, we believe that the aftermath of the Great Recession will present opportunities for growth—even better-than-average growth—to companies that are positioned to exploit them.

As we will see, history teaches us that past periods of slow economic growth have been brought to an end by waves of innovation. Thus, in the same way that economies of the past were resuscitated by technological advances—such as the commercialization of electricity or the invention of the internal combustion engine—today's damaged economy could well get a boost from advancements and breakthroughs in such fields as biotechnology, nanotechnology, material science, renewable energy, defense, and health care.

Even if this happens, however, we do not expect to see a return anytime soon of the kind of profit levels witnessed from 2005 through 2007. As research conducted by The Boston Consulting Group (BCG) shows, most industries earned record-high profits in those years. The rising share and profitability of the financial sector contributed to these profit levels, as did high global growth rates, easy access to pools of cheap labor around the world, deregulation of markets and industries, and lower tax rates.

All these factors, which had such a positive influence on profits in the past, are now likely to go into reverse.

In early 2009, Frank-Walter Steinmeier, then Germany's vice chancellor and foreign minister, told the *Financial Times* that "the turbo-capitalism of the past few years is dead."[1] He laid much of the responsibility on shareholders obsessed with short-term profit making. And among the political elite in Europe, his is not a lone voice. Accordingly, we might see changes in capital-gains tax rates as well as the introduction of incentives that favor longer-term investments and discourage shorter-term gains.

Therefore, if this is the environment in which companies must compete, what of the companies themselves?

Recessions separate winners from losers. While overall profit levels fall within an industry, there can be great variation in profit performance from company to company. Markets consolidate as outperformers strengthen their positions, and default rates spike upward as underperformers drop out. In general, larger companies outperform the others, but some small players can leapfrog their weakened competitors and claim a top-three spot in their particular industry.

Most important, companies that outperform in a recession tend to enjoy a sustained advantage. They tend to retain their performance leadership in subsequent years—in terms of both revenue and share price. Indeed, an index of stock prices, base-lined to 1932 (the trough year of the Great Depression), shows that the average stock price appreciation of the top performers over the subsequent five years was 34 percent greater than the average performance of other companies.

The real question, therefore, is what drives a winning performance in a downturn and the following upswing?

To find some answers to this question, we have dug deeply into the history of past recessions, particularly the Great Depression and Japan's Lost Decade, to learn from the companies that fundamentally improved their competitive positions even during those turbulent times. As you will see, we cite these stories throughout this book and devote Chapter 3 to an analysis of the U.S. auto industry in the 1930s. (For a description of our research and how we chose the companies that we cite, see Appendix A at the end of the book.)

In addition to this research, we conducted two surveys of senior managers in large corporations. The first survey, completed in March 2009, focused on the priorities companies had set for themselves to deal with the rapidly deteriorating economic environment. The second survey, completed in September 2009, focused on companies' expectations for the future development of the world economy. Throughout this book we will refer to these surveys (primarily the September 2009 survey) to demonstrate how our ideas about possible economic developments are supported by many of these leaders. (For more information about the surveys, see Appendix B.)

What our research shows is that the factors that drive the success of the best performers in a downturn are actually similar to the factors that make for success in more benign times. In particular, high performers have strong leaders who take decisive action, act early and with resolve, display courage and a commitment to take the fight to their competitors, show a willingness to rethink the entire business model (they spurn sacred cows), and demonstrate the ability to bring their organizations along with them.

Having said this, today's executives probably have more on their plates than their predecessors did. Certainly the strategic and business challenges are more complex today than they were yesterday—as we explain in Chapter 6.

We believe that the agenda of today's CEO needs to include:

1. Reassessing the challenges and opportunities presented by globalization.
2. Rethinking how businesses are managed for shareholder value.
3. Reorganizing compensation systems to align with the new ethics of business.
4. Redesigning corporate governance to avoid uncontrolled risk taking.
5. Regaining public trust in business.

6. Developing new models for business leadership.
7. Helping the management team to think ambitiously about growth by looking beyond today's tough economic environment.

There is much to worry about. But there are solutions to the problems.

■　　■　　■

History is written by the victors, as Winston Churchill famously observed. So any research that identifies typical characteristics of the outperformers from long-past recessions is prone to survivor bias. Other companies may well have displayed the same characteristic, followed the same strategies—and failed.

So we do not suggest that slavish application of lessons from the past will guarantee success today. But, as we describe primarily in Chapters 4 and 5—but also through Chapter 3's story of the auto companies during the Great Depression—the lessons resonate powerfully over the years. They show clearly that well-managed companies can prosper in tough times and that when the upswing comes, these companies can accelerate faster than the competition and increase their lead.

This line of thought reminds us of another observation from Churchill: "A pessimist sees the difficulty in every opportunity; an optimist sees the opportunity in every difficulty."

In this book, our goal is to help you to understand the magnitude and enduring nature of the changes that have taken place and to offer insights and practical suggestions for seizing the opportunities that will present themselves in the aftermath of the Great Recession.

PART ONE

WHAT HAPPENED AND WHAT HAPPENS NEXT

CHAPTER 1

THE DAMAGED ECONOMY

It is tempting to say that the crisis is over. The "Great Recession," as it is being called, did not turn into a second Great Depression. Unprecedented intervention by central banks and governments averted worldwide economic catastrophe.

And signs of stabilization have appeared: optimistic experts increasingly outnumber pessimistic experts, the slump has bottomed out, and pockets of growth have emerged.

So why not declare an end to this gloomy chapter and get back to normal?

Because, unfortunately, the fundamental problems of the world economy have not yet been resolved. The dependence on heavy-spending consumers (particularly U.S. consumers) remains; many important banks are still weak, and it will take years before they return to full health; and the economic scoreboard shows a drop in economic activity not seen since World War II.

According to recent estimates from the International Monetary Fund (IMF), the world economy shrank by 1.1 percent in 2009. The advanced economies (especially the exporting ones such as Germany, Japan, and Korea) suffered the most, shrinking by 3.4 percent during this period.[1]

But even the emerging economies fared poorly—except China, whose growth rate (buoyed by fiscal stimulus) slowed to 8.5 percent in 2009 from 9.0 percent in 2008 and 13.0 percent in 2007. Russia contracted by 7.5 percent, having grown by 5.6 percent in 2008 and by 8.1 percent in 2007. Brazil fell by 0.7 percent, having enjoyed growth of 5.1 percent in 2008 and 5.7 percent in 2007. And India saw growth of 5.4 percent, down from 7.3 percent in 2008 and 9.4 percent in 2007.

The impact of the crisis on world economies would have been even worse without the drastic measures taken by governments and central banks. Governments mobilized an unprecedented amount of money in an attempt to right their economic ships. Estimates range from a massive $5 trillion to a truly staggering $18 trillion to stabilize the financial sector and $2.5 trillion to stimulate demand in the "real economy"—where the production and consumption of goods and nonfinancial services takes place. The IMF puts the estimate at an impressive 29 percent of 2008 gross domestic product for the advanced economies. Meanwhile, leading central banks have lowered interest rates and taken aggressive measures such as *quantitative easing*—the direct purchasing of financial assets such as government bonds. As a result, the balance sheets of the central banks have grown significantly since the crisis started in the summer of 2007. The U.S. Federal Reserve's balance sheet grew by 229 percent from July 2007 to July 2009.

These measures have arrested a slump that was, until the summer of 2009, looking very similar to the Great Depression of the 1930s. This was the picture painted by Professors Barry Eichengreen of the University of California, Berkeley, and Kevin H. O'Rourke of Trinity College in Dublin in their paper, "A Tale of Two Depressions." Between 2007 and 2009, production and world trade dropped even faster than they did in the Great Depression. The major difference between then and now has been the fiscal and monetary policy and the aggressive measures taken to stabilize the global financial system. In making these moves, politicians and bankers did, in fact, heed the lessons of the Great Depression and the Lost Decade in Japan. In so doing, they were acting on the recommendations of Depression-era economists such as Irving Fisher and John Maynard Keynes. Thanks to these coordinated efforts, a second Great Depression was avoided.

Even so, we need to recognize that the initiatives to "reflate" the global economy amount to an unprecedented and historic experiment. Some of these measures, although discussed theoretically, have not been put into practice before. So the big question remains: Is this the end of the crisis, or will the crisis simply follow a different pattern?

To answer this question, we need to examine the background of the current financial and economic upheaval since it burst into the public consciousness in 2007.

■ HOW IT HAPPENED ■

We all know that a crash in U.S. property prices triggered a leverage crisis in the subprime-mortgage securitization market. This, in turn, triggered a global liquidity crisis, which itself contributed to a solvency crisis among some banks and an increase in the pressure to deleverage. When this led to a further decline in asset prices, the whole cycle repeated itself.

It was inevitable that such enormous financial dislocation would lead to significant collateral damage to the real economy. Falling asset prices and the prospect of an economic slowdown dented consumer confidence. Lower demand and a shortage of credit—because of the liquidity squeeze—combined to drive companies toward conserving cash, reducing output, lowering capital expenditure, and laying off workers. Small and medium-sized enterprises were particularly affected as banks cut back their lending in an effort to stabilize their balance sheets, which, in turn, made a bad situation worse and drove some companies into bankruptcy.

The bottom line: the subprime crisis led to a solvency crisis in the financial sector. This, in turn, led to a recession in the real economy, which further amplified the problems for the financial sector as credit losses increased. And as losses continue to increase and credit tightens, the constraints in the financial system collide with an increasing number of personal and corporate loan defaults that naturally follow when economic conditions deteriorate. The two cycles feed off each other.

If there is one phenomenon that best characterizes the irrational behavior that underpins the crisis, it is the history of home values in the United States. As Robert Shiller, an economics professor at Yale University, has demonstrated, U.S. house prices in any given year up to 1997 had virtually always been within about 15 percent of house prices in 1890, when adjusted for inflation (the only exception being the 25 percent drop between the two world wars). In 1997, though, U.S. house prices started to rise dramatically. In just 10 years, the inflation-adjusted price of a U.S. house doubled. In 2006, at the peak of the bubble, Shiller's index reached 202.9 (in 1890, the index stood at 100).[2]

The increase in U.S. house prices was underpinned by the ready availability of debt, particularly after interest rates were cut to 1 percent in order to stimulate a faltering economy in the wake of the 9/11 terrorist attacks. From 2005 to 2007, additional impetus was provided, first, in the form of aggressive risk taking by highly leveraged financial institutions that funded the unsustainable rise in house prices and, second, by the promotion of artificially low-priced adjustable-rate mortgages. With high risk came high reward, at least initially. As returns from mortgage lending increased, banks came to rely on them to drive up their profits. In essence, this turned banks from agents into principals: rather than fulfilling demand in the market, banks were driving the supply of easy credit.

Underlying all this were three widely held assumptions: that the creditworthiness of borrowers was strong, that investors were sophisticated, and that credit risk was widely distributed.

Unfortunately, these assumptions were seriously wrong.

The Creditworthiness of Borrowers Was Lower Than Expected

The first assumption—that borrowers' creditworthiness was strong—was based on the knowledge that credit losses had, in fact, been relatively limited for years. There was, however, a dangerous circularity to this logic. The belief—held by both lenders and investors—in the creditworthiness of homeowners drove spreads lower. This, in turn, caused marginal borrowers to appear more financially attractive than they really were and made it easier for lenders to justify giving them loans.

Many lenders also believed that the more financially constrained borrowers would not be a problem because they would be sheltered by ever-rising home prices. The introduction of home-equity release products enabled many borrowers to treat their homes as if they were ATMs (automated teller machines).

For those who wanted to look, the information about what was really happening was readily available: the doubling of U.S. house prices in real terms over just 10 years, the fact that consumer debt doubled as a percentage of GDP between 1974 and 2007, and the collapse in U.S. savings rates from around 11 percent in the late 1980s to below zero in 2005.

But lenders insisted on lending to people who could not afford the homes they were buying or who were increasing their debt as house prices rose—leading to rapid growth in the innocuously named *subprime* market.

The Sophistication of Investors Was Also Low

The second assumption—that investors were sophisticated— provided further false comfort. Because they had unprecedented access to data and analytics, lenders and investors were assumed to be exceptionally adept. Advanced financial technology meant that risk could be finely tailored to their specific needs. Bolstered by credit insurance and endorsed by rating agencies, this risk was assumed to be negligible.

Consequently, the capital applied against the perceived negligible risk was minimized, and this allowed for a rapid expansion of this asset class. This modus operandi ignored both the poor quality of the underlying collateral and the enormous increase in bank leverage needed to make money from a business with increasingly thin margins.

Risk Was More Concentrated Than Was Widely Believed

The third assumption was that risk was widely distributed among global investors. Even if credit worsened and analytics failed, so the logic went, the absence of concentrated risk would prevent systemic problems. This belief, more than any other factor, explains why—instead of being wary of a market bubble—people were under the impression that this time things were, and would continue to be, *different*. What seems so surprising is that this bubble came hot on the heels of—only seven years after—the bursting of the dot-com bubble.

Unfortunately, not only was homeowner credit suspect, the market too had misread the risk. In the ensuing panic and resulting liquidity crisis, the safety net of risk analytics and ratings was revealed to be an illusion. When investors realized that the risk was largely concentrated in bank balance sheets, their confidence in the financial system eroded rapidly.

▪ HOW GLOBAL MARKETS ABSORBED ▪ SO MUCH RISKY BORROWING

A critical and related question now begs to be asked: Why did global capital markets grow as fast as they did, and how were they able to absorb so much borrowing that appeared to be—in retrospect anyway—so risky?

The answer lies as much in the banks' economics and investor demand for apparently low-risk fixed-income securities that offered good returns as it does in the insatiable appetite of consumers for debt to fuel their spending.

That the banks had become principals, as opposed to merely agents, played an important role in this bubble dynamic. This is so because they (particularly investment banks) were using the profits from their leveraged investments in these risky assets to mask the deteriorating profitability in their core traditional businesses.

In the early part of the decade, with U.S. Treasury bonds offering low returns for the foreseeable future, Wall Street met investors' demand for new instruments by packaging higher-yielding mortgage debt into (apparently) AAA-rated securities. But the incentives driving the mortgage originators and securities distributors created a moral hazard: their rewards were not aligned with sound credit-underwriting principles or the distribution of assets backed by sound collateral. Credit was granted to noncreditworthy individuals, packaged into securities, and pushed out into the market. And seemingly unlimited investor demand inflated the bubble further.

The impact of this bubble on the profitability of the financial sector was impressive: if discretionary bonuses are added back, the financial sector's share of total profits of the U.S. corporate sector rose to close to 50 percent in 2007—up from levels of between 20 and 30 percent in the late 1990s.

When the asset bubble burst, broker-dealers and many banks found themselves with a significant exposure to assets that they thought were sitting off the balance sheet in special-purpose vehicles. Having leveraged up some 30 to 40 times on cheap debt in order to make the numbers work on thin profit margins, they had minimal equity cover for the significant (unrealized) losses caused by marking the investments down to market value. Counterparty alarm set in, and money markets froze as banks panicked about creditworthiness and liquidity exposures. This led to a race to deleverage, reduce exposures to the interbank markets, and safeguard balance sheets. While banks were the original victims, the contagion spread to the corporate finance markets.

Of course, some observers saw the crisis coming. But however loudly they shouted, their voices were not heard because of the coalition of interests that relied on believing in the continuation of the bubble. We all know about the problems of asymmetry between the employees of the banks—who wrote the business and were well remunerated—and the banks that carried the risk; we know about the mortgage brokers who originated business and did not care about its viability; we know about naive (or greedy) consumers, pushy investors seeking enhanced returns, compromised rating agencies, and shareholders who did not hold management to account; and we also know about governments and central banks that were only too happy to see a long-lived expansion of the economy with low inflation and high employment.

But the opportunity to make money seemed too good to miss—or simply one for which banks felt obliged to keep up with the competition. As former Citigroup CEO Chuck Prince put it in the summer of 2007, "As long as the music is playing, you've got to get up and dance."[3]

All these factors notwithstanding, however, it is not clear that a crisis could have been averted even with a superior "systemic risk" regulator in place (unless that regulator could have reversed global trade imbalances and demographic aging). At a certain point, the crisis was likely inevitable—and, worryingly, as we discuss later, the underlying dynamics remain in place. Financial market structure and regulatory reforms will not be sufficient to address issues that emanate from the real economy. So there is a very real risk that the next bubble will build up and, in doing so, present a renewed danger for the real economy.

Furthermore, some of the underlying dynamics that contributed to the property bubble remain. U.S. trade deficits created excess investable dollars in countries that ran a surplus, and much of it was allocated to fixed-income assets. At the same time, the baby boomers, approaching retirement, put a growing proportion of their savings into fixed-income assets. Not surprisingly, these savings found their way (directly or indirectly) into the U.S. housing market, which was the rare market large enough to absorb the tsunami of retirement dollars and provided duration and risk-return characteristics suitable for these investors.

■ THE BANKING SECTOR WILL ■ TAKE YEARS TO RECOVER

The latest estimate by the IMF puts total losses in mature credit markets worldwide—primarily in Europe and the United States—at $3.4 trillion between 2007 and 2010. In the United States alone, write-offs of $2.0 trillion are expected—equal to about 17 percent of GDP in 2007. This damage is greater than the losses of the Japanese banks from 1990 to 1999, which amounted to $750 billion (in 2007 prices), or 15 percent of Japanese GDP—and has occurred in a shorter time frame and on a global scale. Of the total write-downs that the IMF forecasts will be incurred by banks, only 60 percent have been taken thus far in the United States and only 40 percent in Europe.

As a result, banks have been scrambling to raise capital in order to meet minimum requirements for equity. Despite the substantial amount of capital already raised ($760 billion in the United States alone since early 2007), it seems inevitable that additional capital will be required to keep the banks alive. Even more will be needed if (as the consensus of the G-20 group of largest economies indicates) higher equity rates are implemented as part of new regulations. Estimates by the IMF are grim for 2009–2010: after additional write-offs, U.S. banks will have a net loss of $110 billion, and banks in euro zone countries (those belonging to the single European currency) and the United Kingdom will suffer a net loss of about $140 billion. To reach precrisis leverage levels (a 4 percent ratio of tangible common equity to tangible assets), U.S. banks will need $130 billion in fresh capital, banks in euro zone countries will need $310 billion, and U.K. banks will need $120 billion on top of what has already been raised.

However, if governments and regulators require capital requirements to match those that prevailed during the mid-1990s (a 6 percent ratio of tangible common equity to tangible assets), then 50 percent more capital would be needed. In the United States and all of Europe, the IMF estimates that the demand for fresh equity in banks amounts to more than $1 trillion, applying leverage levels of the 1990s.

In order to stabilize the banking system—which is as crucial for the economy as a whole as it is for the financial sector—a recapitalization is required. This could be achieved by the following actions:

1. Buying assets at inflated prices.
2. Direct capital injections.
3. Receivership and reorganization—the approach that the United States used in the savings and loan crisis in the 1980s and that Sweden used in its banking crisis in the 1990s.

Unfortunately, governments shy away from such direct interventions not only because of the costs involved but also because the approaches—with the exception of the third—involve the transfer of taxpayer money to the shareholders and bondholders of the failing institutions. Only in the case of receivership do shareholders and bondholders lose (some part) of their investment, and taxpayers get the option to claw back some of their money, after successful reorganization and reprivatization have taken place.

So governments typically have opted for a fourth way— muddling through. They have dabbled in asset purchases or guarantees and pursued a bit of recapitalization. Mainly, however, they have relied on making money available at very low rates of interest, allowing banks to earn good margins. And they have crossed their fingers and hoped that the economy will improve enough to pull the banks back from the brink.

For an example of muddling through, we need look no further than the "stress test" applied by the U.S. government in the spring of 2009.

What was the methodology? The government used a model that predicts the losses of a bank as a function of macroeconomic factors: GDP growth, unemployment, and the change in home prices. This was fairly logical. Next, they developed a scenario for how each factor was likely to evolve, starting from a baseline, deteriorating at first, and then slowly improving. After that, they created what they called the "stressed" scenario—a characterization of the worst case. And finally, they applied the stressed scenario to the actual income statements and balance sheets of each of the 19 banks that were to be audited.

This all sounds reasonable, but there was a catch. The scenarios were based on forecasts that were wrong. When the stress test was performed in May 2009, several reputable forecasts were far more pessimistic than the "stressed" scenario assumed by the U.S. Federal Reserve. For instance, in the baseline scenario, the Fed assumed −2 percent GDP growth in 2009 and 2.1 percent growth in 2010. The "stressed" scenario assumed −3.3 percent in 2009 and 0.5 percent in 2010. Remarkably, the annualized and seasonally adjusted first-quarter 2009 GDP loss released by the U.S. Bureau of Economic Analysis amounted to –6.4 percent. Furthermore, in a period when forecasts were corrected downward, the OECD was already predicting in its *Economic Outlook* in March that U.S. GDP would decrease by 4 percent in 2009 and stay unchanged in 2010—an estimate shared by the IMF in its *World Economic Outlook* issued in April 2009. Likewise, the Roubini Global Economics (RGE) monitor predicted a 2009 growth rate of –3.7 percent in April. All of these estimates are significantly worse than the "stressed" scenario assumed by the Fed.

When analyzing the unemployment rate, the situation is similar. The Fed assumed a baseline scenario of 8.4 percent unemployment in 2009 and 8.8 percent in 2010 and a "stressed" level scenario of 8.9 percent in 2009 and 10.3 percent in 2010. But the official actual unemployment rate of 8.5 percent in the first quarter of 2009 already surpassed the assumed "stressed" first-quarter rate of 7.8 percent. For the entire year, RGE estimated—as early as April 2009—an unemployment rate of 9.5 to 9.8 percent, which was much worse than the assumed rate in the Fed's "stressed" scenario. Likewise, in March 2009, the OECD estimated the annual unemployment rate at 9.1 percent. Its 2010 estimate of 10.3 percent matched the assumption in the "stressed" scenario. But, as we now know, unemployment had already reached 10.2 percent by October 2009.

As for housing prices—the last component of the stress test—RGE showed in April 2009 that the cumulative 2009 and 2010 change in housing prices would be at least as large as the Fed's "stressed" scenario of –22 percent in 2009 and –7 percent in 2010.

So for each of the three factors in the government's bank stress-test model, the actual data were significantly worse than the assumptions in the worst-case, "stressed" scenario.

Not surprisingly, given these rosy assumptions, all the banks passed. Indeed, based on these results, only $75 billion of additional capital apparently would be required to restore the health of the system, and nearly all of that could be raised privately. The trillion-dollar capital shortfall mysteriously disappeared.

However, it was not just the wrong macroeconomic assumptions that drove this result. First, the U.S. government's effort was seriously understaffed. The total number of regulators engaged on the stress tests was smaller than the number of auditors who typically would perform a routine audit for any *one* of these institutions.

Second, it turns out that the scenarios were actually *negotiated* among different segments of the U.S. government that had vested interests in the outcome. And the banks, too, *negotiated* their own stress-test results: they were allowed to use their own asset-valuation models—the very same models that had led them into the current situation. Securities were valued using not mark-to-market but mark-to-model, which is more easily manipulated. The Treasury broadened its definition of capital to lower the capital needs. And leverage requirements were set at 25:1, which is substantially higher than most independent observers would have proposed as the correct leverage level for the U.S. banking system.

In short, they—the government, in collaboration with the financial institutions—took a very optimistic view. The primary purpose of the exercise was to reassure a jittery market worried about the debt-laden government's ability to stabilize the financial system. It worked. The markets were reassured, believing that additional intervention would be necessary only if the conditions deteriorated further. Unfortunately, the exercise left fundamental issues unaddressed. The governments chose not to force through debt-for-equity swaps that would have wiped out existing equity holders, forced bondholders to bear part of the costs, and stabilized the system without unnecessary levels of panic.

A Lex column entitled "U.S. Banks" in the June 10, 2009 issue of the *Financial Times* described how a U.S. bank had paid back the so-called Term Asset-Backed Securities Loan Facility (TALF) funds it received from the government at the height of the crisis, and the writer concluded that the major U.S. banks were far from stabilized. According to the writer, in all key indicators—leverage, risk capital, and asset quality—the leading banks are in worse shape than they should be (as recommended by the IMF and other institutions) for the long-term stability of the financial sector. Some observers, such as George Soros, have declared the U.S. banks to be "basically bankrupt,"[4] and some have continued to maintain this point of view even after the strong recovery in the financial markets.

Indeed, the banks, rather than realizing their losses, have chosen to hold onto their assets in the hope that the economy and the housing market will improve. In so doing, they have attained a "zombie" status: they appear to be solvent, but only because they have not acknowledged the deterioration in the true value of their assets.

And for the global economy, there is a problem with zombie banks: they don't make loans.

If the situation is bad in the United States, it may be worse in Europe.

Not only do European banks have a higher share of the nonperforming assets, but they also have written down significantly less than their U.S. counterparts (although accounting conventions for assets and trading books are different across some

European countries), and they generally worked with higher leverage and less equity. European banks still have to take about 60 percent of their write-downs, totaling $800 billion. Furthermore, some major institutions are closely linked with Eastern European banks, considered to be particularly at risk by the IMF in its assessment of global financial stability. Consequently, any breakdown could easily spread across to the European banking system. European politicians have also shied away from executing a stress test for fear it would reveal a major need to recapitalize. They demanded that if the stress test were conducted, the results would have to be kept confidential. European bankers and governments, like their U.S. counterparts, have done their share of hoping that they will be able to recapitalize through cheap refinancing and an influx of new business. This is not good news for the banks' ability and willingness to extend credit. This will hinder the recovery.

It is also likely that the European banks will experience a further brake on their ability to lend. The European Commission has signaled that European banks in receipt of state aid will be expected to shrink their balance sheets substantially and reduce their cross-border activities.

The recent positive earnings news from major institutions in the United States and Europe seems to prove the effectiveness of the hands-off, refinancing-through-the-back-door approach. Low interest rates, the demise of a few players (allowing the survivors to widen their spreads), and active trading have allowed banks to boost their profits. Over time, this will help to restore the capital base. But the jury is still out on whether this will be enough in light of the risk of another wave of credit losses caused by rising unemployment and struggling corporate clients. The profitability of banks will be under pressure for years to come—not least because of greater regulation and a new corporate culture that frowns on risk taking. Unlike bankruptcy—which is resolvable through recapitalization—bad core economics are much harder to address. Given all these factors, we cannot avoid the conclusion that it may take years for the banks to become truly healthy again, especially if the real economy fails to achieve a sustained recovery.

Unhappily, this situation—in which governments and banks refuse to acknowledge the extent of their potential losses and so have failed to recapitalize aggressively—is similar in some ways to the situation in Japan in the early 1990s. The risk is that credit flow to consumers and corporations will continue to be seriously constrained. Indeed, the outstanding credit volume in the United States shrank in mid-2009 compared with the year before. At the same time, credit growth in Europe slowed significantly. While this is in part the result of less demand for credit, the IMF has shown that credit supply shrank by a greater degree than demand in 2009, a trend it forecasts will continue through 2010. This trend is particularly strong in Europe, and the IMF expects lending capacity to shrink by 3.9 percent in the United Kingdom and to grow by barely 1 percent in the rest of Europe.

Shrinking credit is bad news for the growth of these economies given that conventional wisdom says that it takes between $3 and $6 of credit for every $1 of GDP growth. In fact, the level of new credit needed to generate economic growth increases every decade: in the 1950s, a little over $1 of credit was sufficient to generate $1 in additional GDP; the comparable number in the 1990s was $3; and in the last 10 years, it has averaged $5.

■ THE OVERSTRETCHED CONSUMER ■

Ultimately, the most pressing problem for banks, and the world economy as a whole, is the deteriorating left side of their balance sheets—the overleveraged consumer.

Indeed, the backdrop to the Great Recession is an enormous increase in long-term consumer indebtedness not only in the United States but also in several European countries, including the United Kingdom and Spain. Curbing the debt-fueled growth will have a significant impact on economic prospects worldwide. With consumers overburdened with debt and suffering from declining home and investment values, many have no capacity to borrow. And even if they do have some borrowing capacity left, looming job insecurity (witness the steep increase in unemployment) and deflating asset prices will make them less willing to do so. Even in the best-case scenario (with job-creation rates equivalent to the 1990s' boom—something that we feel is very unlikely), it could take until 2014 for unemployment to return to 5 percent in the United States.

The most important consumer in the world is the U.S. consumer. To prove it, simply do the math. Consumption has accounted for 70 percent of the U.S. GDP in recent years. The U.S. economy represented 26.8 percent of the world economy in 2008 and 27.1 percent in 2007. This means that the U.S. consumer is responsible for 18.8 percent of world GDP.

And this is only the direct effect of their consumption. The indirect effect—the so-called multiplier—takes their contribution even higher. Consider the case of toys made in China on German machinery and transported around the world by Japanese trucks and Korean ships. A drop in demand from the U.S. consumer has a significant impact not only on the U.S.

economy but also on its trading partners around the world. This explains why the drop in GDP in exporting countries such as Japan, Korea, and Germany was much more severe than in the United States. It also explains why China—as exports came under tremendous pressure and 67,000 factories (including more than half the toy factories in the Pearl River Delta) were closed during the first half of 2008—initiated a $586 billion economic stimulus program. Therefore, notwithstanding the huge strides made in developing economies, it is a fact that when the United States falters, the world is still inevitably affected. Over time, this will change. For now, though, companies all over the world will feel the effects of the slowdown in the United States.

In 2007, the already-high debt burden of U.S. consumers reached 100 percent of GDP. This was mainly driven by the real estate boom that saw the average price of U.S. homes rise by 70 percent in the period since 2001. Many people bought houses they could not afford, betting on further price increases to pay back their loans and relying on seemingly cheap debt fueled by historically low interest rates. Others took out home equity loans—which allowed them to monetize the rising market value of their homes—in order to fund consumption. The overall savings rate of U.S. private households dropped to –2.7 percent in August 2005, the lowest level since the Great Depression. But there is a view that the credit overhang was caused not only by the real estate boom but also by increasing income inequality and stagnating middle-class real earnings in the United States since 1983. As real earnings fell, middle-class Americans were forced to borrow in order to maintain living standards and pay for health care and education.

The change of fortune has been sudden and precipitous— and the effect on consumer demand has been and will continue to be significant. Between the summer of 2007 and the summer of 2009, U.S. household wealth shrank by an estimated $13.9 trillion, or 22 percent. Meanwhile, the savings rate rose to 5.9 percent in the summer of 2009, equating to a reduction in consumer demand of $400 billion per year. Another factor driving down consumption is that, spurred by job insecurity, consumers are starting to pay back their huge debts.

This is not the first time that we have witnessed deleveraging in an economy. In the Great Depression, the nominal debt of U.S. households decreased by one-third between 1929 and 1933. In 1990s Japan, the credit boom affected corporations but not private households, causing the asset bubble to create a higher debt burden for nonfinancial corporations. The corporations reduced their debt burden—relative to GDP—by about 30 percentage points between 1991 and 2001. In both these severe downturns, the borrowers deleveraged significantly. This time around, given the close correlation between credit growth and consumer spending, it is clear that the implications for future growth in the United States and abroad will be significant. This holds especially true because income and demand were stabilized only by government intervention.

How much consumer deleveraging should we expect in the United States?

A return to the long-term average (coincidentally, the debt level that existed in 1997 prior to the spike upward caused by the recent property bubble) would amount to a deleveraging of $4 trillion. This, in turn, would lead to—depending on the rate of deleveraging—a reduction in consumer demand of up to $1 trillion per year for several years to come. More positive assumptions about the rate of economic growth and inflation translate into estimates of a $2.5 trillion deleveraging, but that figure would still lead to a reduction in consumer demand of up to $600 billion per year over several years. On top of all this, there is the impact of higher unemployment and the declining values of assets such as houses, stock holdings, and pensions— all of which are hard to quantify.

How can the real debt burden of consumers be reduced? There are at least five options:

1. *Continuously paying down debt.* Consumers bite the bullet, reduce consumption, and save money in order to pay down loans. This kind of organic reversion to normalized debt levels would be a time-consuming and painful process. It would take many years, if not decades, and it would create a long-term drag on growth in the real economy.

2. *Selling assets to pay back debt.* A broad liquidation of assets would reduce debt levels—either by paying off debt or writing it down—but it would also reduce the value of assets further. This likely would lead to a domino effect of bankruptcies and insolvencies of both private companies and households. The downward spiral in both the financial and nonfinancial sectors would be exacerbated and cause further asset value depreciation, which, in turn, would increase the need for further deleveraging. And with many households being net borrowers, this solution could not be applied universally.

3. *Defaulting.* In the United States, residential mortgages account for 74 percent of household debt and are mainly nonrecourse loans. Many consumers might choose simply to hand back their houses to their creditors and, in effect, default on their loans. This so-called jingle mail (representing the sound of the returned keys falling through the

mailbox) is happening already. Clearly, a further wave of jingle mail would increase problems for the banks.

4. *Replacing private debt with public debt.* If governments were to replace incurred losses on private debt with public debt—essentially taking on the debt burden of its citizens—consumers would be relieved of the problem of how to manage their personal debt-repayment program. Distressed banks would be recapitalized. The burden of losses would now be borne by taxpayers. While this eliminates excess debt to some extent, it also creates a moral hazard for financial institutions and for individuals. There is also a big question as to how much more debt governments can take on.

5. *Pursuing an inflationary policy.* The return of inflation would lead to a decrease in debt levels in real terms, making it easier for companies and individuals to service their debt. While inflation may be unlikely in an economy driven by credit liquidation, it is not impossible to generate. Governments and central banks, particularly in the United States, might try to trigger an inflationary cycle by being slow to reverse the aggressive monetary measures once the economy recovers—hence the call for "exit strategies" by some experts.

At the time of this writing, all of these options are being pursued in various ways. Even so, there is a continuing risk that the combination of an increased rate of savings, a downward spiral of bankruptcies, and a drop in demand will lead to further unemployment and still lower asset values. Irving Fisher described this phenomenon in his 1933 article, "The Debt-Deflation Theory of Great Depressions." He argued that the need to deleverage leads to pressure on asset prices and income owing to a drop in demand. This, in turn, makes it harder for debtors to repay, amplifying the deleveraging problem still further. (For more on this topic, see the sidebar on Irving Fisher in Chapter 2.)

It is more likely that we can manage a relatively orderly deleveraging process, but the drag on growth in the real economy will still be significant for many years to come. As the example of Japan has shown, an economy can experience two lost decades, even without experiencing an actual depression. We say *two* decades because Japan has actually experienced seven recessions over the past 20 years. Although there were only 19 recessionary quarters, recovery was so slow from each one that over two decades Japan essentially suffered almost nonexistent economic growth. And all this took place against the background of a booming world economy (thanks, significantly, to the U.S. consumer) from which Japan benefited through its export industries.

Today, we face a globally connected economy, and it remains to be seen if other parts of the world economy can find ways to compensate for the sustained drop in demand in the United States.

■ REBALANCING OF GLOBAL TRADE FLOWS ■

As we have said, many countries have run significant trade deficits over the past decade. Deficit countries include the United States (4.6 percent of GDP in 2008), Spain (10.1 percent), the United Kingdom (3.6 percent), Australia (4.9 percent), and Greece (14 percent).

Other countries enjoyed significant trade surpluses—most notably the oil-exporting countries and China (9.5 percent of GDP), Germany (7.3 percent), and Japan (4 percent).

This pattern cannot continue. The deficit countries will be unable to maintain their consumption patterns because they need to rebalance their finances. What is more, government efforts to support domestic demand will become politically unacceptable if they simply benefit workers in other countries.

Ideally, there would be a coordinated international approach to rebalancing trade flows. Deficit countries would endeavor to soften the impact of the downturn at home—and thereby, by default, support the export-oriented countries for some time. And the export-oriented countries would boost domestic demand to compensate for the fall in the demand for their exports—and thereby support the necessary rebalancing of trade flows. Without this kind of cooperation, protectionism surely will result.

To accomplish a rebalancing, some fundamentals of the economic and business models in developing economies may need to change. In particular, developing economies will need to focus more on serving domestic consumers—and make fewer goods for export. For multinationals, globalization could take on new meaning as they focus more on producing in developing countries in order to serve the local domestic markets—countries that, for the past couple of decades, have been viewed by some multinational companies simply as low-cost manufacturing locations rather than as consumer markets.

The surplus countries seem to share the same view: all have initiated major programs to stimulate domestic demand. China launched the biggest program with $586 billion, driven mainly by the fear of social unrest if the growth rate were to drop much below 8 percent. Germany took a similar action, although it committed far less money.

Yet, even with such programs in place, it is not easy to reorient an economy.

Countries such as the United States—which increasingly have shifted toward the service sector over many years—cannot quickly return to a manufacturing-heavy economy. Nor can other countries rapidly change their industry structure. In Germany, for example, five core industries—automobiles, machinery and equipment, chemicals, electronics, and metals—employ 17.3 percent of the workforce. In a relatively benign scenario in which the world economy experiences slow growth over a period of several years, nearly a quarter of these jobs—some 540,000 German jobs (equivalent to 3.8 percent of the workforce)—will be at risk. The sheer number of workers in these export-oriented industrial sectors makes it unrealistic to expect Germany to change its business model to focus on domestic consumption. It would be possible for Germany to increase domestic consumption somewhat and reduce export surpluses to a degree, but not by enough to make up for the demand gap following the deleveraging in the United States and several other countries.

What about China?

Given the size of China, its population (1.3 billion and counting), its cash reserves of $2 trillion (resulting from its trade surpluses of the past 10 years), and the impressive economic stimulus program, many people expect China to succeed the United States as the growth engine of the world economy. There are, however, a number of factors that could militate against this. The biggest chunk of the Chinese stimulus program is aimed at domestic infrastructure projects and the development of new industries, particularly for the creation of export goods, rather than at stimulation of domestic private consumption. The program also has protectionist elements that prevent the participation of foreign companies.

More important is the simple arithmetic. As we have said, the U.S. consumer accounts for about 18.8 percent of the world's GDP. In 2008, the entire Chinese economy accounted for 6.4 percent of world GDP when using current exchange rates. Even at growth rates of 8 percent, it will take years for China to make up for the losses in aggregate demand resulting from the deleveraging process in the United States.

Thus, as important an economy as China is, it will not singlehandedly be able to pull the world out of its economic doldrums.

Olivier Blanchard, economic director of the IMF, sees the rebalancing of trade flows as a precondition for economic recovery and fears that it will not be achieved fast enough to prevent an anemic recovery in the United States. He observes, "Were that to happen, one can imagine various scenarios: political pressure may be resisted, the fiscal stimulus could be phased out, and the U.S. recovery might falter. Or fiscal deficits might be maintained for too long, leading to issues of debt sustainability and worries about U.S. government bonds and the dollar, and causing large capital flows from the United States. Dollar depreciation may take place, but in a disorderly fashion, leading to another episode of instability and high uncertainty, which could itself derail the recovery." And he concludes, "Coordination across countries is likely to be as crucial during the next few years as it was during the most intense part of the crisis."[5]

■ Depression Avoided, Recovery Limp ■

Thanks to aggressive political intervention, it looks like the world will not experience a repetition of the Great Depression. But the underlying problems in the world economy—global trade imbalances, shaky banks, and overleveraged consumers in many parts of the world—place a heavy burden on the recovery. As a consequence, we are likely to face several years of slow economic growth.

IMF research supports this view. IMF experts have analyzed the recessions and downturns of the past 40 years and have come to the conclusion that the recessions that were synchronized across developed countries and were associated with "financial stress" (in other words, banking problems) were two to three times deeper than "normal" recessions and lasted three to four times as long. What is more, the upswings following these financial-stress recessions were slower and weaker than they were after "normal" recessions.

In another study, entitled "The Aftermath of Financial Crises," University of Maryland Professor Carmen M. Reinhart and Harvard University Professor Kenneth S. Rogoff point out that all crises lead not only to a sizable drop in production and employment but also to an average increase in public debt of 86 percent.[6] This combination of factors comes about as a result of political efforts to stabilize the banks and the real economy. This is in line with Japanese experience since 1990. It is also in line with some projections of the U.S. Congressional Budget Office, which estimates that the federal government will run a deficit of $1 trillion each year for the next 10 years—and this figure is based on rather optimistic assumptions about economic growth.

Governments know that these problems have to be addressed. Although inflation may be seen as the simplest solution, it is very difficult to generate in a world of shrinking credit. Accordingly, we expect that the world will take the hard way out: saving and paying back.

This will take a long time.

Kondratiev Waves

The situation we find ourselves in could be characterized as a "winter period" of a Kondratiev wave. In the early 1920s, Nikolai Kondratiev, a young Russian economist and a policy advisor to the Ministries of Agriculture and Finance, became the founding director of the Business Research Institute in Moscow. His task was to monitor the economic situation in the Soviet Union and the major capitalist countries.

Using a broad range of indicators—including long-term movements in wholesale prices, wages, and interest rates—Kondratiev identified three waves of economic development between 1790 and 1920. In so doing, he accurately anticipated the Great Depression of the 1930s. His theory was later picked up by Austrian economist and Harvard professor Joseph Schumpeter, who named the waves *K-cycles* after the Russian economist. But Kondratiev did not live to see his theory win general support: he was executed in 1938 after criticizing Stalin's agricultural reforms. It probably did not help his cause that he predicted that capitalism would survive the Great Depression.

The classic K-cycle is a long wave of economic development, lasting 50 to 60 years, that progresses in four distinct phases:

> *Phase 1, or "spring,"* lasts about 25 years. It is a period of expansion driven by innovation and the implementation of new technology. It produces greater overall prosperity and, eventually, inflation.

Phase 2, or "summer," runs for a fleeting 5 years. In this phase, the period of expansion reaches its peak and then encounters difficulties. In particular, excess production creates a shortage of resources, and the resulting effect—increased costs—leads to lower profits. As a result, economic growth slows down.

Phase 3, or "autumn," endures for around 10 years. This phase is characterized by the first recession in the K-cycle, after which the economy enters a stable period of relatively flat growth. In this plateau period, lower inflation and a positive future outlook encourage people to take on more credit.

Phase 4, or "winter," lasts for about 18 years. It begins with a protracted recessionary downturn—up to 3 years in duration—after the indebtedness of the autumn phase destabilizes the economy. This is followed by a period of up to 15 years of slower growth rates until the next spring phase begins.

What are the driving factors behind these waves of economic development? Economists are divided on the answer. Some argue that the waves reflect changing patterns in capital accumulation or the availability of commodities and food; others contend that wars or social upheavals explain them. But the dominant theory—articulated by Schumpeter—is that technological innovation is the main engine of economic development.

If we add one—possibly two—further waves since Kondratiev's death, K-cycle theorists have identified four or five waves of economic development since the end of the eighteenth century, together with the innovations that drove them.

The first wave, the age of industrial revolution, was driven by the invention of the steam engine and the growth of the textile industry (1780s to 1840s). The second wave was triggered by the emergence of the railway and the growth of the steel industry (1840s to 1890s). The third wave was sparked by the large-scale commercialization of electricity and its development for general use (1890s to 1940s). The fourth wave, which started in the 1940s, came about as the result of the development of petrochemicals and the expansion of the automobile industry as the motor car (invented 50 years earlier) became affordable for everyone.

Some argue that the fourth wave is not yet finished and that the world is in its winter phase—a period of slower economic growth. Others insist that a short fifth phase began in 1980 to 1985, driven by new developments in information technology and telecommunications. According to this view, the world has entered an autumn/winter phase that could last until 2015 to 2025, although there is a strong basis for arguing that the increasing pace of technological change is shortening the cycles.

Whether the world is in its fourth or fifth wave of economic development, however, there is no disputing the fact that it might be in a phase of decline that will last for a number of years.

■ EXECUTIVES EXPECT A LONG PERIOD ■ OF SLOW GROWTH

Given the bleak economic environment and outlook we have discussed, we felt it necessary to move beyond the opinions of economists and other expert commentators to gain a thorough understanding of the expectations and actions of leading companies in the industrialized world. To that end, we conducted two surveys of senior management in large corporations. The first survey, conducted in March 2009, focused on the priorities that companies had set for themselves to deal with the rapidly deteriorating economic environment and sharp fall in consumer spending. The second survey, completed in September 2009, focused on companies' expectations for the future development of the world economy.

With regard to economic growth and the shape of the recession, executives were quite cautious (but not unduly pessimistic) in the March survey. The majority (63 percent) expected a U-shaped recession, with an upswing in 2010 or 2011. The minority, 13 percent, expected a V-shaped recession, meaning a sharper and faster recovery. A sizable group of 22 percent favored an L-shaped recession, similar to that of the Lost Decade in Japan. It came as no surprise to us that Japanese executives were the most skeptical of our respondents—41 percent of them expected an L-shaped recession. This gloomy view may well stem from the fact that Japanese executives have seen all this before, and base their expectations on bitter experience.

In our second survey, we again asked executives about their expectations for growth in the coming years. A striking majority expected a sustained period of lower growth (46 percent expected the aftermath of the Great Recession to proceed in an L-shaped pattern, a further 43 percent expected a U-shaped pattern, and only 10 percent expected a V-shaped pattern). Nearly half of U.S. executives expected an L-shaped pattern, along with 50 percent of Germans and 74 percent of the Japanese, who became more skeptical than they were in March (up from 41 percent)—again, presumably because they have been here before. Higher numbers of respondents in Italy and France assumed a fast return to precrisis levels. In specific industries, those executives working in the energy and utilities industry and the commercial services industry were relatively optimistic (neither industry was much affected by the downturn until now), whereas those working in hotels, restaurants, leisure, and real estate were the most cautious in their outlook.

Because a return to a precrisis level of economic vitality seems unlikely, management teams all over the world will need to reassess their strategies and priorities in order to be ready for the new world of low growth.

And that will be just one of the "new realities" of doing business in the years to come, as we will discuss in Chapter 2.

CHAPTER 2

THE NEW REALITIES

The Great Recession and the upheaval it has caused are truly without equal in the working lives of today's executives and managers. For years, and save only for a few minor blips, executives and managers have enjoyed a long-lasting boom— at least in most developed economies—characterized by growth, increasing profitability, and decreasing government intervention.

But that "old reality" has been fundamentally, perhaps irrevocably altered, so even as managers deal with day-to-day business challenges, they are looking to understand how the postrecession world will shape up. And that is not easy. When you are in the midst of a crisis, it is hard to know which changes are secular and which are merely cyclical. As executives plan ahead they need to ask: What assumptions should we be making, and which scenarios should we be baking into our plans?

We believe that there have been—and will continue to be—fundamental changes to some of the critical components of the global economy. It is too early to say quite how far-reaching and deep these changes could be—or indeed whether all of them will materialize. But we do expect to see some real change—driven by the damage to economies around the world and reinforced by the looming threat of prolonged slow economic growth—in a number of areas: the role of governments; the dynamics of trade; the shape of industrial, fiscal, and monetary policy; the mind-sets and behaviors of consumers and companies; the profitability of corporations; the structure of companies and entire industries; and the importance of innovation.

Complicating the picture is another major uncertainty: Will we see inflation or deflation? For corporate leaders and investors, this is an important question. In a deflationary environment, it will be even harder to achieve tangible growth because the price levers become virtually impossible to exploit.

These potential changes together constitute what we call the *new realities* under which businesses must operate. In Chapter 6 we explore in more detail how some of these realities might shape the managerial mind-set. But first, let us establish what these new realities are and how they might change the competitive landscape.

■ THE RETURN OF THE ■ INTERVENTIONIST GOVERNMENT

Since the early 1980s, there has been a worldwide trend—driven originally by President Ronald Reagan in the United States and

Prime Minister Margaret Thatcher in the United Kingdom—toward liberalization, deregulation, and privatization as governments pushed back the boundaries of the state. This trend gained momentum after the breakup of the Communist bloc in 1989 and the subsequent moves toward more openness in international trade that came to be called *globalization*. One of the main areas of deregulation was in the financial sector, and it was such deregulation that laid the foundation for some of the excesses that have been witnessed in recent times.

However, the process of deregulation and liberalization has halted abruptly. Indeed, it is now clearly going into reverse—a move strongly signaled by the G-20 nations in their 2009 meetings. The financial crisis is forcing governments to become altogether more active and more interventionist. This expectation of more interventionist governments is shared by 75 percent of the corporations we surveyed in the second of our 2009 surveys.

The increase in government activism is driven by a number of factors:

- The desire to continue supporting economies around the world through spending and an expansive monetary policy.
- The aim to reduce a dependency on imports through the "reindustrialization" of the economy.
- The wish to protect domestic financial and business interests from acquisitive foreign corporations.
- The requirement to take ownership of major companies—particularly banks but also failing businesses such as the U.S. automotive companies.
- The pressure to take steps to prevent another global economic crisis through the introduction of new regulations.

These factors are combining in a way that has important consequences for companies and their leaders. We now consider each one in more depth.

The Expectation of Fiscal and Monetary Stimulus for Many Years to Come

Governments and central banks are likely to pursue an expansionary policy for many years to come. They will try to compensate for the drop in aggregate demand that has been caused by the need for consumers and banks to pay back their debts. Some people estimate that consumers and banks need to pay back around $7 trillion across the globe—an amount equivalent to more than 10 percent of global gross domestic product (GDP).

We expect that governments and central banks will continue their efforts to stabilize their economies by funding additional demand, maintaining low interest rates, and continuing aggressive monetary stimulus efforts—following in the footsteps of Japan after its real estate and stock market bubbles burst in 1990. Japan's central bank kept interest rates at very low levels, while public debt increased from 69 percent of GDP in 1990 to an expected 227 percent in 2010.

In their study cited in Chapter 1, Professors Reinhart and Rogoff demonstrated that financial crises are usually associated not only with unemployment and a significant decline in output but also with a substantial deterioration in government finances. On average, across their sample, government debt increased by more than 80 percent in the three years following a crisis.

Given the scale of the current downturn and the unique debt problems in major economies, things could be even worse this time around. In the United States, for example, Alan Auerbach and William Gale from The Brookings Institution expect deficits to average at least $1 trillion per year—equivalent to nearly 7 percent of U.S. GDP—for the next 10 years.[1] This is an observation with which the U.S. Congressional Budget Office agrees.

But governments do not have unlimited capacity to take on new debt. And for countries that were already burdened by debt in the run-up to the financial crisis, this is an issue. Risk premiums for Spain, Greece, and Ireland have already increased. And even the United States has a limit to its capacity to take on new debt as it compensates for the shortfall in domestic savings by depending on foreigners to buy its Treasury bonds. Its most important foreign investor is China, which recently has expressed some discomfort with the huge level of new U.S. government debt.

As the global economy improves, governments will come under mounting pressure to rebalance their budgets. The danger is that this action could push the world back into recession—which is exactly what happened when President Franklin D. Roosevelt attempted to rebalance the U.S. government's budget in 1937. Christina Romer, chair of the Council of Economic Advisers, shares this view. She has argued that many more years of aggressive government spending will be necessary to restore the economy to full health.[2]

Certainly, government spending will be significant for years to come, and this will lead to higher taxes and an additional incentive for some politicians to seek inflation. A broad majority of the executives whom we surveyed expect governments to continue running deficits for many years to come—and 56 percent expect that, as a result, taxes will be higher in the future. Tax increases, in turn, would decrease disposable income and further contribute to the depression of consumer spending—a downward spiral that we described in Chapter 1.

A world in which fiscal and monetary stimulus is needed over many years will have some important implications for companies. For one thing, it will be increasingly important to be close to the government in order to benefit from these programs—whether through lobbying for electrification as General Electric did during the Great Depression or by anticipating where the government will be spending its money.

The Attempt to Reindustrialize

Over the past decade, millions of jobs were exported from the United States and the European Union to rapidly developing economies such as China and India. The backlash has begun, with protectionist calls to repatriate these jobs. And in the United States, President Barack Obama announced the withdrawal of tax breaks for U.S. companies that exported jobs overseas.

More significant, several Western governments seem to be deciding that it is insufficient to base their economic growth on the service sector—and that they need to start a program of reindustrialization. The rise of the "service economy" was a feature of the boom. But a one-trick-pony economy does not work. Recognizing this, some countries are investing aggressively in new industries, including renewable energy and other green technologies.

In the United States, the United Kingdom, and France (three countries where there is much talk of reindustrialization), the manufacturing sector represents around 15 percent of value added—compared with around 25 percent in Germany and Japan.

Over the next few years, we expect to see significant government interest in stimulating the growth of manufacturing through the provision of investment-related tax breaks and training programs designed to develop skills—a trend reinforced by some subtle protectionism that is already starting to emerge. As Lord Mandelson, when serving as the United Kingdom's secretary of state for business, enterprise, and regulatory reform, put it, the country should have "less financial engineering and more real engineering."[3]

The adjustment to wages driven by the Great Recession will support this trend toward reindustrialization because lower wages in Western economies make labor more affordable. Indeed, companies have already begun to take advantage of this newly affordable labor pool. According to *BusinessWeek*, IBM has decided to set up outsourcing centers in low-cost states of the United States instead of establishing more of them in India.[4]

Some 71 percent of the executives in our survey expect governments to push reindustrialization policies. The figures are relatively higher for executives in the United States (83 percent), France (79 percent), and the United Kingdom (66 percent) and lower for those in Germany (59 percent) and Japan (52 percent).

It seems likely that governments will—as they promote a policy of reindustrialization—focus particularly on emerging high-skill and high-tech industries such as nanotechnology, biotechnology, photonics, material science, and green technology. These young industries offer the lure of extremely high growth potential. Supporting them would be a medium- to long-term investment, and the end result could be creation of the leading industries of the next Kondratiev wave of economic development. (See Chapter 1 for a discussion of Kondratiev waves.)

For example, the global market for nanotechnology (the development of incredibly small structures and particles of around one-millionth of a millimeter in size) is already worth around $65 billion, and it is growing at 15 percent per year. Similarly, the global photonics market (optical technologies focusing on microscopic light quanta—the study of which won Albert Einstein a Nobel Prize) reached $70 billion in 2008 and is growing at more than 8 percent per year.

Another hot new industry—the $100 billion so-called white biotechnology industry (which brings living microorganisms such as molds, yeast, and bacteria to industrial use) is growing at 10 percent per year, whereas material science (the development and application of new industrial materials) is already a $450 billion industry that is growing at 5 percent per year. To put these numbers in context, the information technology (IT) industry is forecast to grow at 1.1 percent per year, whereas the chemicals industry is forecast to grow at 2.5 percent per year.

To understand how governments are supporting such industries, take a look at the German government's announcement in June 2009 of an €18 billion research and education development plan. It pledged €700 million for promoting electrical mobility. This initiative aims to bring together green technologies, material science, and nanotechnology in order to develop a high-powered car battery expected to enter serious production in 2012.

Meanwhile, in the United States, states and towns have been promoting green technology. Michigan, an important industrial state, has spent more than $1 billion in the last several years to attract alternative-energy companies, and Toledo, Ohio—a center of glass manufacturing in the nineteenth century—has leveraged the presence of the local university and its innovations in solar energy to pursue the development of solar panel manufacture.

Although governments are promoting reindustrialization, it is not clear that this is an entirely practical policy. Given the living standards and wage levels in most developed economies, the focus will have to be on industries that require a high level of skill and expertise. But not every country can reindustrialize around renewables, nanotechnology, material science, biotechnology, pharmaceuticals, photonics, defense, aerospace, IT, and other highly skilled industries.

Moreover, the risk is that support for these industries will become subject to protectionism as countries fight to control them. Just look at the United States, which imports $1 billion worth of oil each day. Some lobbyists promoting green energy are basing their message on a potential reduction in the country's dependence on foreign oil and on a likely boost to employment. They assert that alternative-energy businesses could create 1.7 million U.S. jobs—albeit over an unspecified time frame.

The Risk of Increased Protectionism

Global trade has grown from less than 10 percent of global GDP during the 1950s to around 25 percent today. But this level could be a high-water mark. Protectionism is becoming a major threat as governments realize that there will be no return to the precrisis level of GDP growth anytime soon. In tough times, it is difficult for politicians to pursue policies that are just as or more beneficial to foreigners (for instance, promoting the demand for imported goods) as they are for domestic voters (for instance, the creation of new jobs).

There are already signs of a beggar-your-neighbor policy. Publicly, leaders may try to distance themselves from protectionist words, but their deeds reflect a different story.

Recessions historically have been associated with a surge in protectionism. During the recessions of the 1980s and 1990s, government investigations designed to counter *dumping*—

whereby companies in one country would sell products in another country for less than the cost of production or the amount they charge in their home market—increased by some 200 to 300 percent. This time around, there has been only a modest increase in the number of antidumping investigations. Global Trade Alert, a free-trade watchdog group, thinks that one reason for this is the ongoing global negotiations over tightening antidumping standards, which reduce the incentives for countries to initiate investigations. It is also a fact that any increase in investigations tends to lag recessions, so the number may yet rise more sharply.

Developing countries have taken the lead in imposing tariff and nontariff barriers—accounting for more than 50 percent of all trade restrictions—despite warnings that even small tariff increases can hurt worldwide growth dramatically. The European Central Bank, in its September 2009 monthly bulletin, pointed out that a 5 percent unilateral tariff increase in a large economy could lower GDP growth by 1 percentage point over four years. And if several economies took such action, the impact would be altogether worse. And therein lies the real risk: a spiral of protectionism.

But modern trade protectionism typically does not take the crudely old-fashioned form of increased tariffs—although Russia and India have introduced such financial penalties on foreign cars and steel, respectively, and there was a well-publicized spat between the United States and China over tires. World Trade Organization (WTO) and European Union rules have forced countries to find more indirect (but often not so subtle) forms of protection.

In February 2009, interest groups in the United States began lobbying for a "Buy American" clause to be added to industries receiving funds from the stimulus package. For example, all public buildings and works projects were expected to use only

U.S.-made iron, steel, and manufactured goods. International criticism has led to the grant of exceptions and amendments in order to comply with WTO guidelines.

Even in its watered-down version, however, the "Buy American" clause is likely to distort trade. Already, local authorities have been conveying the message that they assume that the production of goods takes place in the United States if a company wants to participate in projects funded by the government. This has prompted some Canadian provinces to retaliate, and some non-U.S. multinationals—even those employing several thousand Americans in the United States—are grumbling about protectionist behavior (although they are doing so only in private because they fear even more problems with future contracts).

The U.S. action has led to the adoption of similar clauses in other countries, such as the following:

1. The Chinese government announced a "Buy Chinese" clause in May 2009 for its $586 billion stimulus package. The clause urges government investment projects to buy domestically made products unless products or services cannot be obtained easily in China. In addition, several industries were defined as "core." This meant that, in effect, foreigners were forbidden from participating in the domestic business.
2. The New South Wales state government in Australia has adopted a "Buy Australian" policy.
3. Spain's Ministry of Industry, Tourism and Trade has urged Spaniards to buy more local products.

More evidence of the rise of protectionist tendencies lies in the increased number of bailout packages for companies—especially those in the automotive sector—and the reluctance of governments to fund these automobile company bailouts if they benefit other economies at the expense of their own.

In France, the government controversially announced that recipients of government bailouts in the automotive sector would be required to offer "engagements" or "counterparts." Nicolas Sarkozy, the French president, speaking in the context of the provision of aid to the French automobile industry, said, "It is justifiable if a Renault factory is built in India so that Renault cars may be sold to the Indians, but it is not justifiable if a factory of a certain producer, without citing anyone, is built in the Czech Republic and its cars are sold in France."[5] Although this condition was withdrawn after outcries from the European Commission claiming that the financial crisis should not be used to introduce protectionism, it is realistic to assume that the carmakers will take the hint.

But this thinking is by no means restricted to France alone. Even the nonprotectionist German government—which initiated a generous "cash for clunkers" program benefiting mainly foreign producers of small cars—was criticized by countries such as Belgium, Poland, and the United Kingdom. These countries allege that the German government preferred a failed bid for one of its domestic automobile manufacturers on the basis that jobs for German workers would be guaranteed.

All this happened *before* the full effect of the crisis had reached Europe's labor market. So it is no wonder that the European Commission is worried about the future of the single market. As one commission official put it, "If we can get through the next five years with the single market fully intact, we can congratulate ourselves."[6]

In addition to traditional protectionism, which applies to the flow of goods, companies are being confronted by new forms of protectionism that apply to financial services. The high-growth years were associated with a significant increase in cross-border lending. According to the Bank for International Settlements (BIS), cross-border loans now represent nearly 50 percent of all loans (up from just over 20 percent in 1995). With so many banks under pressure and requiring government support, it is not surprising that governments (and public opinion) are starting to put pressure on banks to stop lending outside their home market. In Greece, for example, the government insisted that the €28 billion support package for Greek banks should not be used to support their Balkan subsidiaries.

Elsewhere in Europe, companies are complaining about the significant pullback of U.K. banks from international lending, whereas in the United Kingdom, companies are seeing similar behavior from foreign banks. In the first quarter of 2009, BIS reported that external claims of all BIS-reporting international banks fell by 2.3 percent. Some 80 percent of this decline was accounted for by a reduction in international lending to other banks.

Given the scale of cross-border lending over the past few years, this systematic retrenchment will have a profound long-term effect. In Central and Eastern Europe, where so many banks are in foreign ownership, the fallout is already visible. The contraction in lending capacity amplifies the deep problems there (especially given the high share of foreign currency–denominated debt), which potentially could trigger a crisis across the region that could be bigger than the Asian crisis at the end of the 1990s. In other countries, reduced access to funds will exacerbate the credit crunch, deepen the recession, and be a drag on long-term growth.

It is not only money that has crossed borders. The high-growth years have witnessed an enormous increase in foreign nationals living outside their homelands—more than 200 million of them around the world. Consider three examples, cited by the Organisation for Economic Co-operation and Development. The proportion of foreign nationals living in Italy rose from 2 percent to 5 percent between 1996 and 2006; in Spain, from 1.4 percent to 10.3 percent; and in the United Kingdom, from 3.4 percent to 5.8 percent. Not all this growth represents economic migration, but a lot of it does. And with economies in crisis across the developed world, the pressure is on to reverse this trend. An unwelcome consequence of any slowdown in economic migration could be an increase in unrest in the poorer nations that have been relying on the export of their (predominantly) young men as a source of foreign earnings through their remittances home.

Rising unemployment puts pressure on governments, forcing them to protect domestic workers at the expense of migrant workers. In the United Kingdom, there was a strike by oil workers protesting the offering of jobs to foreign workers (albeit European Union nationals) by a U.S. contractor to the U.K. operations of a French oil company. The strikers called for "British jobs for British workers." The workers won concessions. And this was after the liberal law allowing easy immigration from Eastern European countries was reversed by the U.K. government.

Such protests, targeting migrant workers, have flared up all over the world:

1. In Greece, anti-immigration protests turned violent, with mobs attacking immigrant groups.

2. In the Czech Republic, the government announced that it will pay foreign workers to return to their native countries; it has committed $3 million to the program.

3. In Malaysia, the government decided to revoke the visas of 55,000 Bangladeshi workers following protests by the Malaysian Trades Union Congress. The decision to revoke visas followed an earlier ban on hiring foreign workers.

4. In the United States, foreign students who typically have stayed in the country after finishing their studies—thus adding to the talent pool—are facing increasing difficulties in doing so.

So, whether it is the application of conditions for state aid, the pressure of public opinion, industrial action, favoritism, the widening of the definitions of "sensitive" industries, the use of "sustainability" as a reason to invest locally, or any of the many other forms of job protectionism, there will be more of it over the coming years.

This trend defies the laws of free trade. There is a broad consensus among academics that free trade generates wealth for all the countries participating in an open market and that protectionism is not helpful for any country. But the political reality means that protecting domestic labor is a high priority, especially in times of crisis. And it comes as no surprise that most of the executives (more than 70 percent) we surveyed expect an increase in protectionist measures.

Only executives in Japan and Germany, the most export-dependent nations of the developed world, are more optimistic. But they run the risk of being severely disappointed.

More Government Ownership of Companies

As part of the efforts to stabilize the domestic economy—and in an attempt to secure jobs, facilitate necessary restructuring, and protect businesses from foreign ownership—governments are becoming active shareholders in many companies, not solely financial institutions. We doubt that politicians will achieve their goals, because governments—at least in the past—have not demonstrated superior skills in running companies.

Nonetheless, given the increased pressure of public opinion and the eagerness of some politicians to be the saviors of last resort, government ownership will become a more common sight. And it is unlikely that governments will dispose of their equity positions quickly once the crisis is over. Experience from the past shows that the denationalization process can take years, if not decades—even in countries that embrace free-trade principles.

In addition to buying stakes in companies, governments will also promote measures designed to prevent foreigners from acquiring important businesses. In France, the government set up a fund designed to help prevent domestic companies from being acquired by foreign investors. In China, The Coca-Cola Company was unable to acquire a local juice manufacturer after the authorities cited competition reasons.

More Regulation

The mandate for a new regulatory regime in the financial sector is overwhelming. In all regions of the world, politicians and regulatory authorities are debating how to avoid a repetition of the financial crisis. They remain concerned about the high leverage ratios of financial institutions, the potential reemergence of highly speculative investors, the damage that can be caused by unregulated financial innovation, and the misalignment between executive pay and long-term performance. The Obama administration has proposed a new regulatory regime; the European Union (EU), BIS, the G-20, and the International Monetary Fund (IMF) all have made their own (variously overlapping) proposals. It seems certain that more regulation of the financial industry will be the result.

A harmonized global regulatory regime is unlikely because several countries—particularly those with strong financial sectors—are reluctant to impose overly strict rules, fearing that they could lose their competitiveness. But financial sectors still will be affected by the efforts to strengthen domestic regulatory regimes. These efforts are likely to bring within the regulatory framework alternative investors such as hedge funds, as well as the previously unpoliced over-the-counter derivatives markets, whose potential to affect the financial system is not matched with a commensurate level of oversight.

Financial institutions will not be the only businesses affected by regulatory constraints. As politicians regain some of the power and influence they lost during the boom years of private enterprise, they will intervene more prominently in a range of industries in order to protect domestic companies, limit competition, and regulate earnings. Obvious candidates for more intense regulation include the energy and health care sectors— both of which attract close public scrutiny.

Health care has already been catapulted to the top of the U.S. political agenda. And given the high and increasing costs of health care, along with huge and mounting government deficits, the United States (and other countries) will need to identify areas where savings can be achieved—for instance, the pharmaceutical and direct-care business. As for energy, the sustainability agenda provides governments around the world with all the excuses they need for intervening in a more proactive way.

All this matters because regulation, while critical to providing appropriate safeguards, is too often a restraint to effective commerce—and therefore growth. And if this seems an overly pessimistic scenario, it is one shared by many business leaders: 81 percent of the executives in our survey share our view.

■ THE EMERGENCE OF ■
THE NEW CONSUMER

Consumers drove the boom—in some countries with a momentum that was turbocharged by excessive debt. And it will be consumers who—through voluntary and involuntary changes to their habits and behavior—will determine many of the new realities of business life in the aftermath of the Great Recession.

In the past, consumers could be counted on to spend an economy out of a recession. But no longer. A whole generation will start to spend less for two reasons: one, because its members either can't or don't want to borrow more; and two, because the times of easy wealth creation in stock markets and real estate are essentially over.

Already, savings rates have been creeping up across Europe and in the United States as consumers have started paying back debt and have kept their hands in their pockets, precipitating a big fall in retail sales. When the U.S. savings rate leapt to 5.2 percent in the fall of 2009, it was the highest level in more than 10 years.

This savings culture reflects the mood of the times. And in the future, consumers worldwide—and especially in the United States—can be expected to:

1. Be more value-conscious.
2. Extend their working lifetimes.
3. Become more conservative.

Consumers Will Be More Value-Conscious

Consumer behavior is changing rapidly, with an emphasis on so-called trading down—that is, shopping for bargains and purchasing lower-cost alternatives to the premium goods they once favored. Value retailers—for instance, Aldi in Germany and Wal-Mart in the United States—have been gaining market share around the world. Wal-Mart's U.S. like-for-like (LFL) sales increased by about 3.6 percent in the first quarter of 2009, compared with three of the largest U.S. luxury department store chains, which saw LFL sales decline by 22 percent on average in the same period.

Value-oriented products have also been enjoying a rise in popularity—something indicated by the slump in sales of bottled water as consumers have elected to drink tap water (even in restaurants). Supermarkets' lower-cost private-label products are taking market share from premium brands. And within the supermarkets' private-label product lines, the value end is performing best of all. Andy Bond, the CEO of Asda, the second-biggest U.K. retailer and Wal-Mart subsidiary, sees a "whole new consumer generation," as reported by the *Financial Times*. "We are moving into an area of the frivolous being unacceptable and the frugal being cool," Bond said.[7]

Bond's view is in line with several consumer studies, including The Boston Consulting Group's annual trading-up/trading-down survey. Ostentatious consumption is shunned even by those who can afford it. Fewer people have the enthusiasm or the confidence to trade up. And the chances of consumers returning to their old ways anytime soon look wildly optimistic. As Bond puts it, "Anyone waiting for things to get back to normal is mad."

The executives we surveyed recognize this—90 percent identified this shift in consumer behavior as the primary challenge facing their company and industry. The new normal will indeed be quite different from the old one.

And this shift will be exacerbated by the severe unemployment we are witnessing in many countries. In the United States, for example, the headline rate of unemployment of just over 10 percent does not paint the full picture. When we consider that the length of the workweek has been reduced for many jobs, more part-time jobs have been added, and many workers have given up looking for work, the real figure may exceed 16 percent. Consumers out of work, on reduced pay, or nervous about their jobs are unlikely to be confident spenders.

Consumers Will Have to Work Longer

Before the crisis, most consumers had already begun to expect that they would have longer working lives than their forebears owing to increased life expectancy, the inadequacy of pension provisions in many countries, and shifts in demographics. Now, they have also come to realize that the combination of fallen property values and much tougher credit terms means that their homes can no longer be relied on as a source of constantly increasing value. Moreover, for those who are nearing retirement today, the drop in stock market values has eaten into their already inadequate pension pots. No wonder that the group aged 50 and above is currently gaining share in the U.S. labor market: they are returning to or staying in their jobs and are taking on more second jobs in a desperate effort to support their debt-repayment programs and to close their personal pension gap. The consequence will be even higher youth unemployment. The high levels of unemployment triggered by the Great Recession (which will continue to feed through for some time as cost cuts take hold) may well help to shape the attitudes of the generation coming into the workforce in the same way that the Great Depression influenced their grandparents and great-grandparents.

Those living on their savings and investments—especially retirees—have been among the big losers as governments and central banks have tackled the credit crunch by reducing interest rates to record lows. Although, as the economy recovers, their dividend income may recover as well, the income they derive from deposits will not.

This is an important trend for business leaders to understand. Why? First, these retired people will spend less. Second, they will rely more on their families for support. Thus, there will be a group of cash-strapped consumers—members of the "sandwich generation"—who will find themselves supporting both their parents and their children. They will divert spending away from anything but the essentials.

Consumers Will Become More Conservative

The media are full of stories about the differences between today's "here and now" generation and an earlier generation whose behavior was shaped by the experience of the Great Depression or World War II—and how these differences are fading fast. These writers are not exaggerating. It is clear that a whole generation will start to spend less because its members will tend to borrow less.

After 20 years of expanding wealth, unbridled consumption, and optimism, the world will see a fundamental shift in attitudes and behaviors. A world that is paying back debt is quite different from a world of infinitely expanding credit. People are becoming more risk averse, and this will have a profound impact on the dynamic and growth of an economy.

In the last recession, young graduates looked to traditional employers and industries for employment—for instance, industrial and consumer goods companies, the civil service, and professions such as medicine and engineering. Given the fundamental shift in the financial industry and in the political climate, less financially rewarding—but (possibly) more stable—employers will once again become more attractive to top talent. Yet even for white-collar workers, the job markets will be tough.

The reduced appetite for risk will also affect the current generation of teenagers. This is the group most likely to suffer the combined effects of fewer job opportunities and the propensity of older workers to continue working later in life (in order to compensate for reductions in their retirement benefits). A prolonged shortage of jobs will shape the worldview of this generation of teenagers. Recent research by Ulrike Malmendier of the University of California at Berkeley and Stefan Nagel of Stanford University has demonstrated that the generation of "Depression babies" growing up in the 1930s was less willing to invest in stocks and expressed more risk aversion.[8] Today's generation of "damaged-economy babies" will be characterized by a stronger propensity to save rather than splurge, less speculation, longer time horizons for investments, and also, perhaps, less entrepreneurship.

Increased Political and Social Tensions

As consumers try to manage the new realities of life after the Great Recession, there will be a concomitant shift in social mood. The period of economic expansion, easy credit, and reduced global tensions since the end of the Cold War created an atmosphere of optimism and confidence. The abrupt economic slowdown, along with the return of protectionism and other forms of economic nationalism, will have a clear impact on the political climate, as follows:

- *Social unrest.* The deeper the economic slump and the greater the additional destruction of wealth and savings, the more tensions will rise. There have already been signs of social unrest in countries such as Iceland, Bulgaria, Latvia, and Lithuania as local economies have slumped. And in China, police chiefs were summoned for a briefing on the potential for social unrest in light of that country's economic challenges.
- *Political instability.* Although government spending will prevent a repeat of the unemployment and poverty of the 1930s, the political stability of the past three decades is at risk because of the magnitude of the crisis.

Social unrest and political instability could drive governments into the arms of some very different policies. In particular, they could promote *fundamental doubts about the free-market economy.* The old faith in the superiority of the free-market model is certainly being eroded—not only in traditionally less free-market societies such as France and Germany but also in Anglo-Saxon countries such as the United Kingdom. Even in

the United States, respected economists favor bank national-
ization in order to prevent the collapse of the banking system.
This change in mind-set—reinforced by domestic political
considerations—could lead to the kind of government intervention and regulation, as well as higher taxes, described earlier in this chapter.

■ A TURN IN THE PROFIT CYCLE ■

During the long years of high growth, companies became
accustomed to reporting rapidly improving quarterly earnings.
As research from BCG shows, most industries earned record-
high profits in the years leading up to the crisis, resulting in the
buildup of cash positions, increased payouts and buybacks, and
intensified merger and acquisition activity. In the United States,
for example, corporate profits reached a record-high share of 13
percent of GDP (compared with 7 percent in the early 1980s).

The rising share and profitability of the financial sector contributed to these profit levels, as did high global growth rates,
easy access to cheap labor, the deregulation of markets and
industries, and lower tax rates. But these years will be remembered as halcyon days because there will be no return to the
profit levels of 2005–2007 anytime soon.

Profits under Pressure

When the financial crisis first struck, many companies sur-
prised the markets by beating analysts' expectations for profits.
They did so by aggressively cutting costs, even as they showed
disappointing sales figures. Going forward, these companies
will struggle to grow profits in the era of low growth. Some 68

percent of executives in our survey think that profit levels in their industry will be lower in the coming years; only 10 percent are confident that profit levels will rise.

There are two main reasons for this shift.

The big reason, of course, is the altogether tougher climate in which to run a business—one marked not only by lower economic growth and excess capacity but also by higher costs resulting from interventionist government activity: protectionism, greater regulation, and higher taxation.

The other reason—and a side effect of the tougher business climate—is that the corporate modus operandi will have to change. Well-run companies will be characterized by solid balance sheets, good cash positions, and strict risk management—all of which will likely contribute to lower profit levels as postrecession prudence replaces prerecession leverage.

Institutional Investors: A Changing Perspective?

The buoyant valuations that some companies enjoyed in mid-2009—up from the lows during the depth of the Great Recession—suggest that investors, far from thinking that the world is entering a new phase of low growth and profits, expect markets to return to precrisis levels. But we do not believe that such a bounce-back is possible. It is more likely that the high earnings and stock market "recovery" came about as a result of fast and decisive cost-cutting measures and that it will be difficult for the market to return to its old highs—unless cheap money allows the buildup of another bubble, whose bursting could be even more risky for the future development of the world economy.

Investors almost certainly will adapt and change their expectations in the years ahead as they come to understand the challenges companies face when operating in a low-growth environment. Not only will dividends become a more important component of value creation (while capital gains, which are driven mainly by growth, will become less important), investors also may prefer less risky investment strategies.

In a recent survey, BCG questioned a broad cross-section of professional investors and market analysts in the United States and Europe. We asked them how they think companies should be responding to the downturn. Their responses suggested a sea change in perspectives and priorities from just a couple of years ago:

Focus on the long term. During the past two decades, many investors became focused on near-term results, notably in relation to growth in revenues and earnings per share (EPS). In light of the downturn, however, investors claim to have shifted away from this short-term focus on earnings toward a new willingness to support management teams that want to manage for the long term. They are giving chief executives permission to focus on doing what needs to be done to create long-term competitive advantage.

This is not to say that careful cost cutting and tight management won't remain critical. But the investors in the survey were adamant that even as companies do what is necessary to secure their financial viability, they should avoid what some called "burning the furniture"—that is, cutting so much that a company damages its future growth prospects—just to meet quarterly EPS guidance. Nearly three-quarters (72 percent) of the respondents in our survey said that they favor companies that make long-term investments to strengthen their competitive position—even if it requires lowering EPS guidance over the next few quarters. As one investor put it, "This is a unique time in history to gain share and keep it."

View the downturn as an opportunity. Investors worry that well-positioned companies are not being aggressive enough in pursuing the opportunities available to them. Eighty-four percent of respondents to our survey agreed with the statement that the Great Recession represented a "once-in-a-lifetime opportunity" for some companies. And nearly 40 percent wish that those companies would be more active in seizing the moment. "Not enough companies are recognizing that this environment is an opportunity to align your forces and use strategic positioning and assets to better your position in the market," said one investor.

Adopt a value mind-set. Another shift in perspective concerns the nature of investors' priorities. Typically, different investors have distinctive investment styles with different priorities and preferences for growth, risk, the best uses of cash, and the like. During the boom, for instance, it mattered whether a company's investor base consisted mainly of growth investors, growth-at-reasonable-price (GARP) investors, or value investors—because each group had its own criteria for valuing a company, and each was attracted to different types of companies and different sectors of the economy.

If our survey is any indication, however, more and more investors are shifting to a value mind-set. Thirty-six percent of respondents said that they have become "more value-oriented" (in contrast to just 4 percent who said they have become "more growth-oriented"). Of the respondents who said that they had modified their investment philosophy since the downturn, 9 out of 10 said that they had become more value-oriented.

One consequence of this migration to value is that investors are far more focused on a company's balance sheet, liquidity, and cash situation. As one investor we interviewed put it, "Now, it's only about cash flow." Another added, "I pay more attention to cash flows, especially to the security of those cash flows."

Of course, experience shows that investors change their mind-sets as quickly as the stock market changes direction. So, since March 2009, when the market began to recover and when there was talk of "green shoots," the pendulum may have swung back. But we remain convinced that the results of our survey signal what can be expected once the fundamental shifts in the economic environment become more starkly visible.

Stakeholders, Not Shareholders

In the era of high growth, shareholders were a dominant force, and their demand for value creation was paramount and prompted a headlong rush for profits. However, in an era of low growth, investors will have to get used to diminishing influence and power. The notion of a "socially responsible" company—one that balances the interests of its owners with those of its staff, local community, and other stakeholders—will continue to rise higher on the corporate agenda.

The robust discussions about "dividends versus jobs and pensions"—where shareholders are pitched against employees—and the very vocal involvement of political leaders suggest that there may be fundamental changes in the future. The culture of a company will assume a new importance. It is no accident that some companies are starting to offer shorter workweeks and sabbaticals to their employees rather than cutting jobs alto-gether. Not only do they wish to preserve their skill base, but they also wish to act responsibly—and to be seen as acting responsibly in the aftermath of the Great Recession.

■ THE SHAKE-UP OF INDUSTRIES ■

Recessions typically accelerate the reshaping of industries by exposing ineffective business models and weeding out under-performers. And given the pressure on profitability that we have just described, the Great Recession will be no exception. The sluggish recovery and long period of slow growth certainly will provoke the restructuring of companies and industries.

The Demise of Poor Business Models

Companies with poorly grounded business models will face sig-nificant pressure and either adjust or be forced to exit the mar-ket—witness the stress being placed on the automotive industry. Tough economic times tend to reinforce structural weaknesses. The newspaper industry, for example, is suffering from a double whammy. For years, it has been struggling as the Internet has transformed the way people access and use media—and now, in addition, it is facing a decline in advertising, which is forecast to recover only slowly. The same holds true for the postal sector: the shift away from mail to electronic distribution gained significant momentum in 2009 and industry leaders, considering this more than a mere cyclical change, don't expect companies to return to precrisis levels of spending on direct mail.

Companies with structural weaknesses are more likely than well-grounded companies to default on their financial obligations. Over the last few quarters, in fact, we have begun to see a rise in corporate default rates. The default rate among speculative-grade companies has jumped from 2.4 percent in the second quarter of 2008 to 11.5 percent in August 2009. Moody's Investors Service, the ratings agency, expects the rate to peak at 13 percent over the next few quarters.

Arcandor, the German retail group that recently filed for bankruptcy, provides a good example. The retailer had been struggling for a decade and nearly went bankrupt in 2004. Arcandor's business model had remained virtually unchanged despite fundamental shifts that had occurred in the market in which it operated. Its long-standing slogan—"Everything under one roof"—had worked well in the absence of large-scale specialty and discount retailers. However, the strategy failed to be effective as shoppers moved toward specialist stores selling expensive goods on Main Street and discounters with lower costs offering goods at rock-bottom prices. The Great Recession proved to be the final nail in the coffin. Saddled with high rents negotiated during the boom, the company also had to contend with collapsing revenues.

An unfocused product strategy has plagued many other companies during the Great Recession, including Woolworths in the United Kingdom, the general retailer that filed for bankruptcy in 2009. In the United States, Eddie Bauer also filed for bankruptcy in 2009. The company, which was a victim of high debt levels—having let its debt be syndicated, traded, and owned by very aggressive hedge funds—suffered because consumers stayed away from its large-footprint mall stores and because the retail promotional crossfire to woo back customers drained the company's margins. Now, after restructuring, Eddie Bauer is back in business.

Increased Consolidation and Changes in Leadership

In the new era of low growth, many companies will be forced to engage in merger and acquisitions (M&A) activity to survive. Excess capacity, resulting from the fall in consumer demand, will force many companies to either merge or exit some businesses. There will be other pressures too—including the emergence of new technologies and industries and the efforts by governments to protect mature domestic champions—that will present formidable challenges to lead-footed companies in mature industries.

This new M&A activity will lead to a transformation of some industries. The pecking order of companies within industries has often been disrupted and rearranged in previous recessions. During the last downturn, 8 of 10 industries experienced shake-ups. One-third of the companies in the top 10 dropped off the list during the crisis, whereas less than half that number lost their top-10 positioning over the period of the ensuing upturn.

This time the changes will be even deeper and more fundamental.

The Race for Innovation

In past recessions, the level of innovation, creativity, and new-product development went up. Several economists see revolutionary innovations—such as the railway, the automobile, and the computer—as the driving force behind the long waves of economic development first identified by Kondratiev.

As discussed in Chapter 1, the current crisis may signal the end of one such wave, with many of the industries that drove the development of the last decade now reaching maturity. New industries will shape the next economic expansion: biotechnology and new energy technologies—to name just two—will lay the foundation for future growth and prosperity. Companies will need to understand which innovations will drive the next wave of economic development and how they can ride that wave. Such an understanding will also help politicians to identify where to direct their fiscal stimulus.

■ THE BATTLE BETWEEN DEFLATION AND INFLATION ■

In this chapter, we have set out many of the most important facts of business life in the new era of low growth—which we term the new realities. But there is another potential new reality that should not be ignored: the question of whether we will see either deflation or inflation. This question takes on greater significance in an era of low growth because the general economic environment can make it either easier to raise prices (inflation) or more difficult (deflation).

It is not easy to know whether, in the aftermath of the Great Recession, deflation or inflation will prevail. In the first quarter of 2009, the consensus was that deflation would assert itself. Toward the end of the year, however, there was a growing view that inflation or even hyperinflation would be the dominant feature of the global economy. In our executive survey, about half the respondents said that they expected deflation to be the dominant feature in the short term. Over the medium term, however, nearly three-quarters said that they expect to see inflation.

This deflation-inflation debate is no mere academic diversion. Knowing which of the two might assert itself and understanding their different effects will be an all-too-real new reality for business managers. Answering the question correctly could offer huge opportunities.

We think that the jury is still out on what might happen. Let us quickly summarize why we think both options are possible.

In Chapter 1, we discussed the need of private households, corporations, and financial institutions to pay back their debt—to deleverage. This pressure is amplified by the drop in asset values, mainly stocks and real estate, which intensifies the pressure on debtors to make repayments. The devastating power of such deleveraging was described by Irving Fisher in "The Debt-Deflation Theory of Great Depressions" (see the sidebar at the end of this chapter).

The goal of the massive government and central bank intervention in the major economies of the West has been to avoid a repetition of such a debt-deflation spiral. It would have had extremely grave implications for the economy, employment, and social stability. In late 2008, the Bank of England's Monetary Policy Committee saw that the "risks to inflation have shifted decisively to the downside."[9] The IMF was similarly pessimistic at that time, stating that "another downside risk [to the already negative scenario of lower worldwide growth] relates to growing risks for deflationary conditions in advanced economies."[10]

It is true that deflation must be avoided because it would increase the current debt burden. It would also, by triggering alarm about falling prices, lead to a reduction in consumer demand. The lessons from Japan during its Lost Decade in the 1990s (and beyond) should be a warning to policymakers today: notwithstanding major public spending, zero interest rates, an undervalued yen, and a fast-growing world economy, Japan did not escape recession and continuing deflation.

The unprecedented levels of new government debt and the aggressive lending by the central banks have—until now—prevented this from happening. But the first implications of the deleveraging activity are visible.

In normal times, the unconventional stimulus measures taken by governments and central banks over the past year would have been highly inflationary. An increase in the balance sheet of a central bank typically would lead to higher credit growth—and inflation—if supply does not pick up. Milton Friedman, the economist, described this as "too much money chasing too few goods."

In the aftermath of the Great Recession, though, the so-called money-multiplier process has collapsed. As a result, an increase in the supply of money from central banks has not led to more credit—and therefore inflation. It has merely helped to stabilize the existing volume of credit in the economy.

The trouble is that the global economy—and, particularly, highly leveraged economies such as the United States—needs inflation in order to facilitate the efforts of companies and consumers to reduce their debt levels. Some observers argue that once national economies return to a stable growth path, central banks and governments will have little reason to prevent or control inflation.

What is certain is that the task of reversing their aggressive monetary stimulus policies will be difficult. As the Federal Reserve Bank of Dallas noted in a working paper, "As the real economy improves, tightening must be 'measured' enough not to destabilize still fragile confidence and financial markets but also fast enough not to allow inflationary expectations to rise too much. This will be particularly difficult if the source of demand expansion was itself a rise of inflationary expectations associated with quantitative easing. And to all this must be added the risk of political pressure being applied by governments worried about the cost of debt service on rapidly rising debts."[11]

The return of inflation would lead to a significant drop in bond prices for governments and corporations, which would imply much higher interest rates. This, in turn, would have a negative effect on the economy, potentially causing another recession and increasing the risk of deflation. Central banks will have to walk a very narrow line, and as they do so, the global economy may experience a period of increased volatility of price levels.

Another factor affecting the inflation-deflation debate is the price of raw materials, particularly oil. Given the structural factors of shrinking supply and increasing demand (especially from the emerging economies)—even in a lower growth environment—it is quite possible that higher oil prices will become the norm. But this is not likely to lead to inflation because, given the weak economy, companies will not be able to pass on the higher costs to consumers. Companies thus will face reduced profits, and consumers, paying more for oil, will have less money to spend on other goods and services—a recipe for deflation.

It is impossible to say how the battle between deflation and inflation will play out in the real economy in the years after the Great Recession. Even if inflation returns to the fore, the chances are that deflation will make a regular reappearance, as it did during Japan's Lost Decade. This duality is a new reality that managers will have to come to terms with in the years ahead.

■ THE VICIOUS CIRCLE TO SLOWER GROWTH ■

There is no doubt that the world economy faces a long period of lower growth. As we stated in Chapter 1, real GDP growth in the Western economies will be around 1 percent annually in the years to come compared with an Organisation for Economic Co-operation and Development average of 2.5 percent over the last couple of years.

This era of low growth will create a series of new realities for business leaders, and these, in turn, will pose an additional burden on future growth.

Of course, innovations will offer companies—and the global economy—a way to a prosperous future. But they will take time to emerge, and it might take some years until the world regains its momentum, despite the stabilizing impact of the emerging economies.

Having said all this, it should not be assumed that things will be "all bad all the time" for everyone and that every company will suffer. Indeed, there will be many opportunities for companies to gain market share. But more than ever, winning and losing will depend on defining and executing the right strategies. As we explain in the next chapters, differentiation will be the key for companies to build the best chance of prospering in the aftermath of the Great Recession.

IRVING FISHER'S DEBT-DEFLATION THEORY

Just a few days before the Wall Street crash of 1929, Irving Fisher, the great Yale economist, had confidently talked of a "permanently high plateau" of stock prices. He thought they would never fall. And after the crash, he believed that a recovery was just around the corner—putting his money where his mouth was and losing much of his personal fortune (prompting John Kenneth Galbraith to observe that losing $10 million was "a sizable sum even for an economist").[12] Later, reflecting on the tragedy of the Great Depression, Fisher came up with his famous debt-deflation theory.

Prefacing the theory, Fisher analyzed the nature of instability and equilibrium. He distinguished between two sorts of cyclic tendencies: "forced" cycles (such as seasons) and "free" cycles (not forced from outside but self-generating, like waves). Fisher concluded that "exact equilibrium [...] is seldom reached and never maintained for long. New disturbances are [...] sure to occur."[13]

It was in this context that Fisher considered the features of business, economics, and investment: overproduction, underconsumption, overcapacity, price dislocation, maladjustment between agricultural and industrial prices, overconfidence, overinvestment, oversaving, overspending, and the discrepancy between saving and investment. These are all factors that help to explain business cycles.

But Fisher singled out two other factors—indebtedness and deflation—as the biggest reasons for booms and busts. And the two factors could be linked by a chain of events. As he put it:

Assuming, accordingly, that, at some point of time, a state of overindebtedness exists, this will tend to lead to liquidation, through the alarm either of debtors or creditors or both. Then we may deduce the following chain of consequences in nine links: (1) Debt liquidation leads to distress selling and to (2) contraction of deposit currency, as bank loans are paid off, and to a slowing down of velocity of circulation. This contraction of deposits and of their velocity, precipitated by distress selling, causes (3) a fall in the level of prices, in other words, a swelling of the dollar. Assuming, as stated above, that this fall of prices is not interfered with by reflation or otherwise, there must be (4) a still greater fall in the net worths of business, precipitating bankruptcies and (5) a like fall in profits, which in a "capitalistic," that is, a private-profit society, leads the concerns which are running at a loss to make (6) a reduction in output, in trade, and in employment of labor. These losses, bankruptcies, and unemployment lead to (7) pessimism and loss of confidence, which in turn lead to (8) hoarding and slowing down still more the velocity of circulation. The above eight changes cause (9) complicated disturbances in the rates of interest, in particular, a fall in the nominal, or money, rates and a rise in the real, or commodity, rates of interest.[14]

Fisher said that the combination of overindebtedness and deflation is devastation. "The two diseases act and react on each other," he said. The first leads to the second, "and, vice versa, deflation caused by the debt reacts on the debt. Each dollar of debt still unpaid becomes a bigger dollar, and if the overindebtedness with which we started was great enough, the liquidation of debts cannot keep up with the fall of prices which it causes. In that case, the liquidation defeats itself. While it diminishes the number of dollars owed, it may not do so as fast as it increases the value of each dollar owed."

Fisher identified two ways to get out of an economic depression. One is the natural and long way, through bankruptcy, unemployment, and starvation. The other way—artificial and quick—is to "reflate the price level to the average level at which outstanding debts were contracted by existing debtors and assumed by existing creditors."[15] This is precisely what governments and central banks around the world are trying today.

PART TWO

WHAT TO DO

CHAPTER 3

EVEN IN THE WORST OF TIMES

Recessions—and the ensuing period of low growth—affect all companies. But it falls to a company's leaders to define not only how well the company gets through a difficult environment but also how its competitive position can be improved for the future.

History shows that structural shifts in the pecking orders of industries occur more often in difficult times—and these shifts endure for a long time. So the fight to sustain company performance during a downturn is not just about short-term survival—it is also about long-term positioning in the industry hierarchy. This is clearly a battle worth fighting.

If we want to learn about how companies can thrive in the damaged economy that follows a massive economic crisis, there is no better place to look than the Great Depression. The 1930s was a period of enormous disruption. The upheavals created new economic realities and shook up whole industries. Even in the worst of times, though, some well-run companies not only survived the crisis in good shape but also thrived in its aftermath.

Many companies that outperformed their peers in the Great Depression continued to do so for many years afterward—and by a substantial degree. There is no more dramatic an example than the U.S. automobile industry, with General Motors (GM) and Chrysler building the foundations for four decades of future success. In Chapters 4 and 5, we offer a detailed description of the defensive and offensive strategies that underpinned the success of high performers during past downturns. To set the scene, though, let us look at what happened to U.S. automobile manufacturing during the Great Depression.

Like today, the automotive industry was among the most adversely affected in the crisis. From 1929 to 1932, sales of new automobiles fell by 75 percent—and automobile companies had a combined loss of $191 million in 1932 ($2.9 billion in today's money), or 25 percent of industry sales. This compared with profits of $413 million in 1929, or 14 percent of industry sales. The highly profitable luxury end of the market virtually disappeared. The lower-priced segment grew from 40 percent of sales in 1929 to 80 percent of sales in 1933 and remained at 60 percent through the upturn and beyond. As a result, half the automakers closed down.

Although it may seem ironic to look to the U.S. automobile industry for examples of how to thrive in a damaged economy—given its performance during the Great Recession—the truth is that the performance of Chrysler and GM during the 1930s stands out. GM delivered a profit in every year of the Great Depression, and Chrysler incurred a loss in only one year.

Prior to the Great Depression, the automobile market had been split three ways. GM and Ford Motor Company each enjoyed a one-third market share. Several smaller companies shared the final third. GM and Chrysler grew their market shares by a staggering 15 and 19 percentage points, respectively. In contrast, inaction combined with some poor choices significantly hurt Ford's position and permanently damaged the smaller competitors.

What differentiated GM and Chrysler from their competition was their superior understanding of how to adjust to the new realities presented by the Great Depression and their ability to look for advantage. In other words, they employed the strategic basics of both defense and offense.

■ GENERAL MOTORS: A QUICK, DECISIVE, ■ AND COMPREHENSIVE RESPONSE

It is not that GM anticipated the Great Depression better than any of its competitors. According to Alfred P. Sloan, president and later chairman of GM from 1923 to 1956, "It would be unfair to claim any particular prescience on our part; no more than anyone else did we see the depression coming. . . . [W]e simply learned how to react quickly. This was perhaps the greatest payoff of our system of financial and operating controls."[1]

That system enabled GM to quickly mount a defense to the changing economic conditions in the 1930s. The company acted decisively to cut costs: mothballing plants, laying off workers, rapidly scaling back production in its middle-market and high-end brands, and reducing the breakeven point on its lower-end Chevrolet brand by a third. To reduce inventories,

GM aggressively cut prices by as much as 70 percent on its expensive cars—a move that would have been unthinkable under any other circumstances. Because GM had limited backward integration (ownership of suppliers), it was able to keep fixed costs low and transfer some volume risk to suppliers, enabling GM to scale down production quickly when demand collapsed. The company used the same engine and parts across different brands to further reduce inventories and create flexible capacity. And it merged its sales forces across middle-market brands to make the sales force more effective and better use sales capacity.

At the heart of GM's success during the Great Depression was its decision to realign its product offering to fit the needs of a consumer base with less money to spend—creating "a car for every purse and purpose," as Sloan put it. GM expanded aggressively into the low-priced car market by shifting production from high-end brands to Chevrolet, its high-volume discount brand. GM spent more on advertising for Chevrolet and offered financing as a way to create an attractive package for customers at a time when banks were not lending. As a result, GM gained share and commanded a higher price than Ford could for comparable products.

■ CHRYSLER: MAKING THE BIG THREE ■

The Chrysler story shows how a decisive attack strategy can work even in the toughest of times. For Chrysler, the Great Depression was a game-changing period during which it rose from startup status to one of the "Big Three" U.S. automakers. Founded in 1925, Chrysler had merged with Dodge, a much larger company, in 1928. Although the merger improved its scale, Chrysler still had just an 8 percent share of the market when the Great Depression hit.

Like GM, Chrysler had chosen to undertake little backward integration, giving it more flexibility than most of its rivals and allowing it to cut costs rapidly when the Great Depression hit. Chrysler also executed the sort of basic measures that companies still follow today: as sales declined in 1930, it closed plants, laid off workers, and reduced administrative expenses by nearly one-third that year.

Driving down costs, even in a crisis, is not easy. Indeed, executives often plead that their (or their department's) needs are special in order to get approval for a budget increase. This is exactly what happened at Chrysler, and Walter Chrysler had to take a creative approach—as the following story illustrates—to get his senior managers to accept the seriousness of the company's situation and to make realistic budget proposals.

Walter P. Chrysler met with his chief lieutenants in early 1930 and insisted that they reduce costs in their departments by 30 percent. Most of his executives, however, proposed spending increases instead. Engineering wanted budget increases to develop new products, the sales department argued that it needed additional resources, and K.T. Keller [president of the Dodge Division of Chrysler] pleaded for funds to upgrade machinery and equipment. Annoyed by their responses, Chrysler asked B.E. Hutchison, the treasurer, to bring him the company payroll book, which listed all of Chrysler's employees. Walter Chrysler then proposed, in a half-serious way, that they lay off everyone in the last one-third of the book. His lieutenants returned the next day with concrete proposals for the reductions Chrysler had demanded.[2]

What truly differentiated Chrysler, however, was its focus on improving efficiency—which would be a competitive advantage under any circumstances. Attempting to compensate for its scale disadvantage in relation to the "Big Two," Chrysler increased its production efficiency by 50 percent. The assembly lines for Chrysler's Plymouth brand reached production levels of 90 cars per hour in comparison with 60 cars per hour at both GM and Ford, which enabled Plymouth to realize the highest profit per unit of any discount auto brand at the time. Although Plymouth had half the sales volume of Chevrolet, it generated 70 percent more profit per unit.

In addition to managing costs effectively, Chrysler also made vital moves to support the top line. Understanding that sales in a severe recession were more likely to come from a budget vehicle, Chrysler had the courage to open new dealerships and expand its advertising and marketing support (thanks to lower advertising rates) for Plymouth, its discount brand. As sales of more expensive brands plummeted, Plymouth sales surged.

Even while it successfully coped with the Great Depression, Chrysler kept its eye on the long term. Chrysler saw that the nationwide highway-expansion program, undertaken as part of the New Deal, would create a demand for faster, more powerful cars. Accordingly, the carmaker continued to invest in research and development during the tough times. It was the first manufacturer to use wind-tunnel testing as part of a design and engineering process that produced more aerodynamically efficient cars. Chrysler's Airflow design and semi-unit-body construction innovations quickly became the industry standard.

Chrysler was managed by a powerful leader. But Walter Chrysler had also built a strong team around him. And it was this bench strength that allowed the company to advance so effectively on so many fronts.

■ FORD: HURT BY HIGH COSTS ■ AND INFLEXIBILITY

As the automobile company that had pioneered high volume and low prices, Ford should have been well positioned for the Great Depression. However, its indecisiveness and inflexibility resulted in declining sales and a 12 percentage point loss in market share. Ford moved from being a contender for market leader to a weak third place. As the most vertically integrated company in the industry, Ford bore the full financial impact of the decline in sales because of its high fixed production costs. Ford's lax accounting and poor business management made cutting costs difficult. In fact, since it was unable to control costs, Ford tried to increase its prices in the midst of the Great Depression.

Ford also fell afoul of a new reality of the Great Depression—one that shows signs of returning today. Unlike GM, which purchased foreign automobile manufacturers so that it could produce entire cars in the country of sale, Ford manufactured parts in the United States and then shipped them overseas to be assembled. This practice made Ford vulnerable to the rise in protectionism. Ford was hit with tariffs of nearly 100 percent on certain parts.

To add to its difficulties, Ford—caught short by Chevrolet's introduction of a V6 engine in 1928—found itself behind the innovation curve at the start of the Great Depression. In an attempt to catch up, Ford rushed a new V8 model to market in 1932. However, the new model was poorly positioned for the value-conscious Great Depression market—it was both more expensive and less reliable than its competitors.

Ford survived the Great Depression, of course, but not without scars. It took years for the company to recover some of the share loss that it suffered in those turbulent years.

■ THE REST OF THE MARKET: ■
ALSO-RANS

Virtually all the smaller companies competed in the expensive or midpriced segments of the market. They were highly exposed to sharp drops in sales as demand fell away. They were slow to cut costs and introduce low-priced models. Apart from Chrysler, the small players either went out of business or lost so much market share that they could no longer compete effectively. Packard, a luxury brand, did not introduce a midpriced model until 1935.

The year 1937 saw the creation of the most unlikely combination when Nash Motors merged (presumably for misguided reasons of synergy) with Kelvinator—a refrigeration and appliance company—and created the hot-water car heater and a vacuum gear-change system. But with little market share and a substantial scale disadvantage, the company was unable to exploit its inventions.

By the mid-1950s, unable to make up the ground they had lost during the Great Depression, none of the smaller brand names remained as stand-alone automobile companies.

THE GREAT DEPRESSION: A BRIEF HISTORY

"Gentlemen, you have come 60 days too late. The depression is over."

With those optimistic words, President Herbert Hoover welcomed his guests—a delegation of banking officials and religious leaders concerned about rising joblessness—to the White House in June 1930. The U.S. economy was indeed showing signs of stabilization at the time, and the Harvard Economic Society even had predicted an upswing during the second half of 1930. After the Dow Jones Industrial Average fell 36 percent from September to November 1929, it then experienced a "dead-cat bounce" (a short-lived rise following a sharp decline) of more than 50 percent growth over the following six months. But, as we all know now, the worst of the Great Depression was yet to come.

The Great Depression is a cultural touchstone for many reasons: it was the longest and deepest recession in modern times. In the United States, real gross domestic product contracted by 26 percent between 1929 and 1933, and consistent growth returned only with the start of World War II. The financial meltdown that triggered the economic collapse affected Americans very directly, more so than in any other financial crisis. More than 9,000 banks (20 percent of the U.S. total) failed in the 1930s. These failed banks accounted for around 10 percent of total U.S. household savings. What is more, the Great Depression was more globally interconnected than any downturn before or after. Economies around the world faltered and fell, and as governments sought to defend their domestic markets with protectionist measures, global trade dropped by nearly two-thirds (from $2.998 billion in January 1929 to $992 million four years later).

The four years after the crash of 1929 were among the bleakest in economic history. Industrial output in the United States declined by nearly 50 percent. Businesses were faced with exceptionally difficult conditions as consumption fell by 25 percent. As a result, corporate profits fell 131 percent, and the value of the Dow Jones Industrial Average declined 89 percent. The unemployment rate rose from 3.2 percent in 1929 to 25 percent in 1933 and remained stubbornly high throughout the decade—in 1939, it was still 17 percent. (Driving this, in part, was a persistent deflationary cycle, as described by Irving Fisher in his debt-deflation theory, which we discussed in Chapter 2.)

With the election of Franklin D. Roosevelt in 1932 and the adoption of the New Deal policies starting in 1933, government fiscal and monetary policies turned from being concretionary in nature to expansionary. Prior to the Great Depression, government expenditure amounted to 9 percent of GDP; by 1939, that share had grown to 16 percent. Although economic conditions began to improve quickly from the 1932 trough, recovery was far from steady. In 1937 and 1938, the U.S. economy entered a recession again as a result of efforts in 1937 by the federal government to rebalance its budget by letting payments to World War I veterans (a form of fiscal stimulus) expire and by beginning to collect Social Security payroll taxes for the first time. Only in the buildup to World War II was growth finally sustained.

In the end, the Great Depression ushered in more changes in society and government policy than any other era. In its wake, savings rates increased as both corporate and personal levels of indebtedness declined. Frugality became a new norm.

As the worst downturn since the Great Depression, the Great Recession will usher in many similar new realities. As Mark Twain famously said, "History does not repeat itself, but it often rhymes"—echoing the past more closely than we might wish.

CHAPTER 4

DEFENSE FIRST

The story of the automobile industry during the Great Depression illustrates the old maxim that a good offense is built on a strong defense. Companies following this path are far more likely to prosper in a low-growth economy. They can build advantage over their slow-to-react or indecisive competitors—who realize too late that they will not be rescued simply by a revival of the economy.

The Great Recession forced companies to cope with the deepest downturn since the Great Depression. And once again, it was the outperforming companies that responded early and decisively. Having stress-tested their businesses, these companies acted the fastest to protect themselves from downside risk, enabling them to safeguard their financial fundamentals and ensure liquidity and stability.

Businesses across different industries and regions were affected differently in terms of when and how they felt the impact of the crisis. For some companies—those least affected—the best response proved to be a program of actions not so very different from business as usual. Faced with shrinking demand but manageable costs, they endeavored to coordinate preserving their balance sheets and managing costs with improving the top line, primarily through smart pricing strategies. But for the worst affected companies, nothing short of a complete corporate turnaround was required—and this necessitated a swift and aggressive cost-reduction strategy to preserve their viability.

In the aftermath of the Great Recession, companies now must adapt to an economic recovery that will be as slow as the downturn was deep. Companies that can stabilize themselves and adapt quickly to the new realities we have discussed will find that the damaged economy presents some new opportunities. The evidence from past recessions suggests that with many competitors weakened, companies deploying the right offensive strategies can surge ahead for a long time to come.

However, in a damaged economy, defense must come first. In such an environment, weak business models will be revealed, and weak companies will find themselves under disproportionate pressure as margins are squeezed and profits drop accordingly.

In Chapter 5 we will talk about going on the offensive—how strong companies with solid business models must start thinking about differentiation to gain market share in a world where everyone competes for their piece of the slow-growing pie. But first, in this chapter, we will see how companies practice the sort of defense that can get them through the worst of economic times and continue to serve them well as conditions improve slowly. Such companies aim to do three things:

1. Protect *financial* fundamentals.
2. Protect *business* fundamentals.
3. Protect revenue.

In highlighting these strategies, in this chapter and the next we will draw on our analysis of three recessions from the past 80 years: the Great Depression, the U.S. stagflation of the 1970s, and Japan's Lost Decade in the 1990s.

We will examine in some depth the stories of a handful of the strongest performers of these periods, including such well-known companies as General Electric (GE), IBM, DuPont, and Procter & Gamble. We will also look at companies that offer very specific lessons, such as RadioShack, F.W. Woolworth Company, McDonald's, and U-Haul. Examples from Japan include Shin-Etsu Chemical, Nitto Denko, Asahi Breweries, and Seven-Eleven Japan. We will also return to the stories of the automakers that we profiled in Chapter 3.

■ PROTECT FINANCIAL FUNDAMENTALS ■

First on the list of good defensive moves is to protect the financial fundamentals.

Protect Your Cash Position

Even companies that survived the worst of the downturn relatively unscathed need to keep an eye on their cash position. Our survey of business leaders shows that nearly all companies are taking at least some action to protect cash, regardless of how hard they were hit in the recession.

However, few companies are prioritizing actions to protect cash or taking a comprehensive approach to cash management.

Only 27 percent reported that managing cash flow was one of their top three priority areas in 2009, making it sixth of 10 priority areas. As a point of comparison, 39 percent said that expanding capacity was one of their top three priorities, and 36 percent put innovation in their top three. For 2010, our respondents told us that managing cash flow was as low as eighth of 10 priorities.

This relative lack of concern about cash flow is surprising given the fragile status of both the credit and equities markets. A return of volatility in these two markets can be fatal for companies in a weak cash position. Even companies with strong cash positions can be caught off-guard by economic fluctuations given the still-shaky status of the economy. As the saying goes, "Cash is king." And in unstable times, companies that do not pay close attention to their cash position will find themselves flirting with danger.

Credit markets are far more stabilized now than they were in the depth of the financial crisis, but the status quo is fundamentally different now. In recent years, commercial loans outstanding—a measure of the amount of lending to businesses— had been growing at more than 10 percent annually in both the United States and Europe. In mid-2007, year-on-year growth in total U.S. lending peaked at 25 percent.

Looking back now, of course, we can see that this level of growth was unsustainable. Since the third quarter of 2008, growth in commercial lending has turned negative in both the United States and the United Kingdom, and it has been stagnant in euro zone countries. While this decline is driven in part by companies paying down debt in the face of lower demand and strained balance sheets, a major driver is a reduction in the amount banks are able and willing to lend. Lending standards have tightened dramatically and have yet to ease despite government exhortations. What is clear is that the Great Recession is forcing companies to face a new reality in terms of their cash conservation. In the face of this tightening, the norms of the past decade—characterized by holding low levels of cash and high levels of debt—will not return soon.

Renegotiate with Suppliers

The financial crisis shifted most major economies from a track of low inflation to lower or even negative inflation. So it is a good time for companies to take a second look at their supplier arrangements and renegotiate in order to benefit from falling prices.

The retailer F.W. Woolworth Company did precisely this during the Great Depression. It had long maintained a wide roster of suppliers—which allowed it to search for the best deals and regularly renegotiate for better terms—but in 1931, it reduced contract periods from 6 months to 60 days. With prices falling owing to deflation, these shorter contract periods allowed Woolworth to negotiate price reductions even more frequently. As a result of this and other measures, Woolworth was able to decrease its costs by an amount greater than the drop in revenues it experienced between 1929 and 1933, and thereby protect its bottom line.

Postpone Spending until You Have Secured the Core

As we will explain in Chapter 5, the current climate may be a good opportunity to invest in new initiatives, but not if the cash position of a company is unstable. At times, it may be necessary to slow down or postpone spending outright in order to stabilize cash positions. This is what General Motors was forced to do during the Great Depression's double dip in 1937. In 1935, GM responded to the upturn in auto sales by using its strong cash position to invest in a new generation of automobile assembly plants that were more efficient because they used cutting-edge technology. When the economy went into reverse in 1937, GM suddenly found itself overexposed. Taking decisive action as it had at the start of the Great Depression, GM was quick to postpone its capital expenditure. Only in 1939, when the worst of the Great Depression was over, were the new assembly plants completed.

Focus on Inventory Management

With rapidly changing economic conditions, it is essential to keep inventory decisions in line with economic forecasts, market dynamics, and changes in the macroeconomy. Two-thirds of companies responding to The Boston Consulting Group's September 2009 survey reduced their inventories during 2009, and an equal number are planning to do so in 2010. But focused inventory management is not just a matter of reducing inventories. It also requires synchronizing inventories to the shifts in the external environment—as the following story demonstrates.

RadioShack, the consumer electronics retailer, was faced with significant inventory management challenges in the 1970s because of the nature of its business model. With a chain of thousands of stores selling identical products, RadioShack needed to maintain substantial inventories yet still achieve high turnover.

The challenge was made more complex by the fact that 40 percent of RadioShack's merchandise was sourced from Japanese suppliers. This meant that two important macroeconomic trends of the time significantly complicated RadioShack's ability to manage its inventory: the fluctuating exchange rates between the U.S. dollar and the Japanese yen, and rising inflation in the United States.

To minimize its exposure to these risks, RadioShack closely synchronized its inventory decisions with its economic forecasting, and in 1977–1978, it was successful in getting ahead of economic trends. (Incidentally, a surprising number of companies in our survey paid scant attention to external economic indicators, and even fewer "baked" these indicators into their operating processes in the form of early-warning systems.) When U.S. inflation picked up in the first half of 1977 and the U.S. dollar began to fall relative to the yen, RadioShack responded by increasing orders from its Japanese suppliers. This, of course, meant running up high inventories. But the combined impact of rising inflation and a weakening dollar could have driven up RadioShack's costs by more than 10 percent per year. So, by stockpiling inventories at an opportune time, RadioShack was able to contain its costs.

Given the heightened risk of inflation in the medium term owing to uncertainty and concern about the "exit strategies" of governments from their stimulus measures, the RadioShack story provides an important lesson for companies today. Inventory management is not just a matter of cutting; it is also a matter of proper forecasting and tracking—and linking to a view on macroeconomic developments.

Reduce Debt Levels

Despite net debt repayments in recent months, many companies are still overleveraged. Thus, for some companies, paying down debt may be a necessity rather than an option. In BCG's September 2009 survey of business leaders, 69 percent of the respondents reported that their companies reduced overall debt levels in 2009, and 71 percent planned to do so in 2010. This seems wise, given that new debt is difficult to obtain and has become more expensive owing to heightened default risks driving interest rates higher; 66 percent of our survey respondents reported that financing was more expensive in 2009 than in 2008, and 68 percent said that it was less available.

Paying down debt may be easier said than done. Thus, taking multiple steps to protect financial fundamentals can help.

In the early 1970s, McDonald's took advantage of the low cost of borrowing to expand its long-term debt from $43.5 million in 1968 to $353 million in 1974 in order to finance a rapid expansion. Yet when bond yields began to increase in the latter half of the 1970s, McDonald's used its strong cash position to pay down that debt rather than issuing dividends. By the time the prime rate reached 20 percent in 1979, McDonald's had returned to a relatively normal debt-to-asset ratio without having to sell assets or raise more equity.

■ PROTECT BUSINESS FUNDAMENTALS ■

Shin-Etsu Chemical is well known in Japan for preparing for downturns while the economy is enjoying an upturn, and vice versa. Of course, given the helter-skelter performance of the Japanese economy over the last 20 years, such preparation is perhaps not surprising. Nevertheless, in 1990, while the Japanese economy was enjoying prolonged strong performance, the new CEO of Shin-Etsu, Chihiro Kanagawa, launched a review of the business that resulted in cost cuts and a major divestment of noncore businesses in order to improve the strategic focus and efficiency of the company. While the fashion for most Japanese business was to develop large and diversified companies, Shin-Etsu recognized that maintaining lean and focused operations would give it the best chance of success.

In practice, this strategy resulted in Shin-Etsu's plastics division focusing on one type of commodity plastic—polyvinyl chloride (PVC). Meanwhile, its competitor, Mitsubishi, continued to invest in five different kinds of commodity plastics through the 1990s. With its single-minded focus on PVC, Shin-Etsu was able to develop market leadership and therefore create a scale advantage, while at the same time it used its expertise with PVC to develop new and better products and manufacturing processes. During the 1990s, Shin-Etsu was known for having one of the leanest operations of all global PVC manufacturers. One factory produced 2 million tons of PVC per year with only 200 staff; by contrast, its competitors employed 2,000 people or more to produce the same amount of PVC.

Shin-Etsu's decision to focus on a lean advantage early in the 1990s led to sustained success, resulting in a 126 percent increase in earnings before interest and taxes (EBIT) and a 4.6 percent gain in market share by 2000. The average EBIT of its six closest competitors in the specialized chemicals industry grew by only 18 percent in the same period (1990–2000).

Things were going well for Shin-Etsu in 2000, but when the dot-com bubble burst, Japan entered another recessionary period. To protect its business fundamentals, Shin-Etsu restructured again, eliminating 10 percent of its workforce. True to its countercyclic philosophy, Shin-Etsu also invested capital in developing new manufacturing capabilities, preparing it for the upturn.

By first protecting business fundamentals, Shin-Etsu was able to use its position of strength to take more aggressive actions throughout the Lost Decade. With its focus on PVC, the company opened new factories in the United States and Europe and undertook joint ventures with Shell, Elf, and AkzoNobel to capitalize on their capabilities in the manufacturing process. By 2003, Shin-Etsu's profit level and market capitalization (indexed to 1991) were, respectively, 50 and 168 percent greater than the average for the specialty chemical industry.

Shin-Etsu's success was the result of a sustained focus on protecting business fundamentals. There is nothing particularly profound about Shin-Etsu's individual actions, and they are things that any company can do. What is most noteworthy, perhaps, is not only the resolve with which Shin-Etsu's leaders acted but also the way, while playing a strong defense, that they prepared a potent offense.

Drive Down Costs

Nearly all companies took some easy, short-term measures to cut costs during the Great Recession, but few companies are now taking long-term actions. While 77 percent of the respondents to our survey said that their companies had cut administrative expenses in 2009, fewer than half took long-term actions to address production—such as reducing capacity, improving efficiency, or doing more outsourcing. But slow economic growth means that it is increasingly important to look toward longer-term cost-reduction strategies. Chrysler's decision to achieve significant production efficiencies during the Great Depression shows how effective timely action can be in driving advantage.

Although cost cutting is most effective when pursued early in a downturn, it is never too late. Two successful Japanese companies in the Lost Decade demonstrate this point: Takeda, a pharmaceutical company, and Nitto Denko, an electrical components manufacturer.

The Japanese pharmaceutical industry performed very well in the 1980s, growing 50 percent through the decade. But once the Lost Decade began, the market stagnated: pharmaceutical industry revenues grew by only 5 percent between 1990 and 2000. Accustomed to the quick growth of the 1980s, most pharmaceutical companies (including Takeda) were highly diversified and maintained high cost bases. Starting in 1992, Kunio Takeda, Takeda's CEO, recognized that lower growth was a new reality that could not be avoided and initiated a transformation of its cost base that lasted a decade. Takeda was helped further by its ability to develop multiple blockbuster drugs and by its strong position in the United States.

Takeda's first cost-reduction initiative in 1992 was the restructuring of its research and development program. The company's researchers had long focused on experimental scientific research. Now, however, they shifted to more focused, business-oriented research. Takeda found this approach to be not only an effective way of achieving faster results but also a good way to reduce costs.

After Takeda succeeded in reorganizing its R&D, it started to offshore some of its production in 1995. By closing many of its Japanese factories and opening new ones in countries with lower labor costs, such as China and Ireland, Takeda was able to achieve significant cost reductions. Over the following 10 years, the share of labor in Takeda's costs of goods sold declined from 38 percent to 17 percent.

Through its major restructuring moves—along with smaller efficiency improvements—Takeda was able to reduce the number of employees by 47 percent between 1993 and 2003 and to improve the productivity of those who remained. Takeda de-layered its sales organization and moved from having the low-est sales productivity in its industry to the highest. It also insti-tuted a merit-based salary structure starting in 2003, with compensation closely tied to performance at all levels of the organization. Takeda's board members were not immune from these changes. Over a decade, the size of the board was reduced by 65 percent, and board members were subjected to the same merit-based compensation policy as everyone else in the company.

Takeda's achievement in reducing its cost base is evident in the steady improvement in its margins throughout the decade. Despite a stagnant market, Takeda's margins improved from 12 percent in 1992 to 20 percent in 2003. And between 1991 and 2003, the company's earnings grew 164 percent more than the average for the Japanese pharmaceutical industry.

Takeda's success and the uniqueness of its actions are espe-cially apparent when compared with its closest competitors. Most of Takeda's rivals took markedly different paths in the Lost Decade.

Some of the Japanese pharmaceutical companies suffered from bloated R&D organizations, a reliance on seeking new blockbuster drugs, and leadership structures that did not actively try to bring down costs. Companies unable to repeat their blockbuster successes tended to get stuck with a high cost base, and this resulted in a steady decline in profitability. By 2003, Takeda had become the market leader, with EBIT more than three times greater than that of its main competitor.

Meanwhile, in Japan's high-tech sector, revenue growth had been slow but steady throughout the Lost Decade, minimizing the imperative for companies to reduce their cost base. When the high-tech-sector downturn hit in 2001, industry revenue fell 24 percent in a single year, with profits down 70 percent. Yet, in that same year, Nitto Denko, the fifth-largest player in the industry, reported revenues and profits down only 3 and 45 percent, respectively. Key to mitigating the impact of the downturn was Nitto Denko's rapid implementation of cost-reduction initiatives, which were completed in six months. Some savings came from quick wins in such areas as warehouse space leasing, but much of the savings came from a deeper restructuring, shifting the company to organizing around profit centers and projects. Within two years of its restructuring, Nitto Denko's EBIT margin more than doubled, far exceeding the performance of its competitors.

Making decisions to reduce costs for the long term is critical for protecting business fundamentals. But at the same time, these cost cuts must be done in a way that protects the core. Empirical evidence shows that companies that cut costs late in the day have a tendency to overreact—not merely cutting the flab but also cutting deep into core operations. Previous downturns are littered with examples of significant labor retrenchment made deeper by late starts—and this recession has been no different, as evidenced by the soaring unemployment figures. Given that such broad-brush approaches can compromise the core of a business, it is instructive to look at alternative approaches.

In the Great Recession, some companies have gone about labor force reduction in far more subtle, well-thought-out ways. These companies have opted to reduce pay or hours, give employees a retainer while they are on furlough, or move skilled employees to lower-skilled jobs in order to retain talent. Such refined strategies were not commonplace during the Great Depression. However, even back then, GE and IBM stand out as examples of companies that took a different approach.

When the Great Depression hit, GE's management was quick to make deep cuts, but it did so in a considered and disciplined fashion. Closely mirroring the drop in sales, the company cut labor costs by 14 percent in the first year of the downturn, eventually reaching a reduction of 62 percent in the trough year of 1932. In comparison, Westinghouse reacted more slowly, reducing labor costs by only 7 percent in 1930 and reaching 59 percent by 1932. Not only was GE faster, but it also took a more sophisticated approach than merely reducing head count. In order to retain as much of its talent as it could and maintain its competitive advantage in the long term, it shortened the workweek, cut wages, and shifted skilled employees to lower-skilled jobs rather than lay them off, as Westinghouse did.

By 1932, GE had laid off fewer employees than Westinghouse yet had succeeded in making larger cuts in average employee compensation. The decision to keep talent within the company helped GE to improve its rate of innovation later in the 1930s and positioned it to benefit from new opportunities as the economy started to recover. As a result, GE's performance far surpassed that of Westinghouse.

IBM's management never conducted mass layoffs during the Great Depression. Wages were cut from 1931 to 1934 in order to reduce costs, but IBM's president, Thomas J. Watson, insisted on retaining talent by maintaining the company's workforce. Watson even introduced a range of employee benefits—such as life insurance, survivor benefits, and paid holidays—in the Great Depression years. This not only kept workers productive and happy but also helped to attract talent from outside the company. Together with a crucial decision to maintain production capacity through the downturn, Watson's determination to maintain the strength of IBM's workforce was instrumental to his company's success during the period of economic recovery after the Great Depression. When businesses began expanding again and federal government programs grew in the middle to late 1930s, IBM had the capacity to fill new orders while its competitors struggled to rebuild their capabilities.

This same determination to use innovative employment schemes to cut costs and, at the same time, keep talent in the company was reflected in the actions taken by KLM, the Dutch airline, in the Great Recession. In mid-2009, reacting to a drop in revenues, KLM asked 2,000 of its pilots to volunteer for jobs as baggage handlers, "hospitality agents," and machine operators—which enabled the airline to save money by hiring fewer temporary workers.[1]

Maintain a Flexible Business Model

Maintaining a flexible business structure allows for quick adjustments to changing economic conditions. Designing a flexible organization at the start reduces the likelihood of having to make difficult cuts down the line. One obvious way to accomplish this is to avoid a vertically integrated business model. At its extreme, a fully integrated model means that a single company controls not only the manufacture of products (or delivery of services) but also their distribution and sale. But choosing not to integrate assumes that certainty of supply or quality is not of such overwhelming importance as to dwarf all other considerations.

As we related in our story of the U.S. automobile industry, this was a key reason for the success of GM and Chrysler. Limited backward integration at GM and Chrysler enabled them to scale down and then later scale up production, with much of the risk borne by the suppliers. To maintain a flexible organization, GM even adopted a policy that no more than 33 percent of parts would be manufactured internally. At both GM and Chrysler, maintaining this flexibility provided the added benefit of allowing them to easily shift production between different types of vehicles, enabling them to switch the focus to their discount brands during the Great Depression.

Flexibility also emerged as an important contributor to success during Japan's Lost Decade. Many of the companies that prospered outsourced production and developed flexible labor structures. Clothing manufacturer and retailer Uniqlo was one of the first clothing companies to outsource production to China. It also increased its use of part-time and temporary workers, thereby developing a more flexible labor structure and making labor costs even more immediately variable. By 2003, 82 percent of Uniqlo's labor force was accounted for by temporary or part-time workers, a far higher percentage than its competitors.

■ PROTECT REVENUE ■

As many companies can attest, and as we have discussed, the Great Recession has had a significant impact on consumer behavior. Consumers are cutting spending on nonessential items, deferring major expenses, buying products at promotional prices, and shopping around to find the best deals—as reflected in the large-scale consumer surveys BCG undertook during 2009. More than 70 percent of respondents in the United States, the European Union, and Japan said that they were taking all these actions. As we observed in Chapter 2, there has been a strong shift from trading up to trading down.

Businesses should not expect a quick return to precrisis levels of spending. Several major macroeconomic trends have affected consumer behavior in the downturn, and they will continue to have an impact through the slow upturn.

First, unemployment, which has risen dramatically in many countries, will increase as more companies respond to the prospect of low growth, and will likely stay high for some time to come. And of those still working, many have shifted to part-time jobs. Second, substantial deleveraging will continue—particularly among consumers as they pay down debt. Third, consumer credit will remain difficult to obtain, as financial institutions continue to cut back credit card issuance and other loans while raising fees.

With this as the context, what should companies be doing?

Cut Prices—Once a Cost Advantage Is Achieved

Consumers are expecting highly competitive pricing. With the consumer price index entering negative territory in the United States and the euro zone countries, price cuts are now the norm.

Looking to the medium term, though, there is a greater risk of inflation. Although BCG's survey of business leaders found that only 52 percent of respondents believe that inflation will occur in the short term, 73 percent think that inflation will appear over the medium term. For companies subscribing to the belief that the risk of inflation is high in the medium term, the case of McDonald's in the 1970s demonstrates how acting early to reduce costs pays off over time. After reorganizing its supply chain in the 1970s to reduce costs, McDonald's was able to reduce prices in 1978, a year when its competitor Wendy's increased prices by 14 percent to cope with inflation.

Although the obvious response to increased consumer price sensitivity is to reduce prices, businesses should do so only if they enjoy a cost advantage. Cutting prices without a cost advantage undermines margins and potentially leads to a destructive price war. Furthermore, just cutting prices without first taking the necessary precautions to cut costs may simply encourage customers to make their purchases earlier than planned—at a lower margin. Take the example of the "cash for clunkers" programs in the United States and Germany. These programs led to a sharp increase in auto sales during the summer of 2009. Some analysts estimate that as much as 50 percent of the sales increase came from consumers who had planned to buy at a later time, which presents the risk of a drop in demand further down the road.

As the case of Maytag in the 1970s demonstrates, making hard choices when it comes to costs can make for easier and better choices on pricing. Maytag—a leading home appliance manufacturer—successfully reduced its product price point in the inflationary environment of the 1970s. But before dropping prices, it first launched an aggressive cost-reduction effort, beginning in 1975.

Maytag adopted three sets of actions to achieve these cost reductions. First, it reduced the number of parts required in its products by using new manufacturing technologies. (Attention to detail really matters; for example, shifting to a new heat-application process eliminated the need for 13 bolts used to attach a water filter, thereby saving $4.3 million a year.) Second, the company launched a $60 million capital expenditure program to improve manufacturing efficiency at its plants, which included the adoption of computerized production-line technology and robotics. Third, it reduced its input costs by diversifying its supplier base—notably by shifting to imported steel.

Known for their quality and longevity, Maytag washing machines sold for a $70 premium (about 20 percent) over competitors in the mid-1970s. But with the cost reductions, Maytag was able to reduce its prices. Consumers responded well, and Maytag's share of washing machine sales increased by 5 percent between 1969 and 1979. In a stagnant market growing at a mere 1 percent, Maytag's increase in market share allowed the company to hold profits and margins steady.

Employ Strategic Pricing

Pricing is a key strategic lever whatever the state of the economy. But this lever can be particularly valuable when times are tough. It is not always necessary to lower the actual price point on a product; it is often possible to lower the perceived price point without sacrificing revenue.

One common tactic is to remove features and slim down products—a move that many food producers have made recently. Another is to unbundle product and service offerings. This gives customers the option to buy more or less, or to split a purchase into two lower-priced elements. A third tactic is to lock in customers and then sell them additional higher-margin products and services. A fourth tactic is to increase prices and discounts. Research shows that consumers are more responsive to higher prices with greater discounts than to low prices. (In Chapter 5, we profile IBM's pricing strategy during the Great Depression. It encapsulated many of these themes.)

For many companies, these pricing strategies are routine, and are used regardless of economic trends—think of airlines selling upgrades to economy-class passengers or technology companies unbundling hardware and software platforms. But some companies, when facing a crisis or economic downturn, may not realize that opportunities exist for strategic pricing. These companies must review their pricing structure to see where advantages exist.

A good example of finding price advantages is U-Haul, the truck rental company. During the 1989–1992 recession, U-Haul adopted a lock-in and sell-up approach. As the downturn worsened and customers became more price sensitive, U-Haul's margins started to suffer. It urgently sought alternative ways to manage the downturn, and discovered a lucrative adjacent market in the sale of high-margin add-on supplies for moving—such as cardboard boxes, tape, and other packaging materials. Once U-Haul had locked in customers with the truck rental, it was able to leverage its position of convenience to sell the add-on supplies at a premium. The impact was dramatic: in an industry with an average operating margin of 3 percent, U-Haul's margin grew to 10 percent.

In the Great Recession, many companies have engineered a downshift in the value and the prices of their products. One food maker's response was typical: in the autumn of 2008, it introduced a new Ecopack product—a slimmed-down yogurt container with less packaging and less yogurt—and charged a lower price. But while the price tag was lower, the new yogurt packages actually cost consumers €0.06 (4 percent) more per kilogram.

■ AFTER DEFENSE, THINK OFFENSE ■

Surviving a downturn—whether the Great Depression or the Great Recession—is not enough to win in the low-growth economy that may follow. After attending to the basics—protecting the financial fundamentals, the business fundamentals, and revenues—executives should look for areas to attack. This is where companies can make the greatest strides when accelerating in a slow-growth economy.

CHAPTER 5

GO ON THE OFFENSIVE

In sports, a victory may be built on strong defense. However, no team can put together a winning season without an effective offensive strategy, too.

It is no different in business.

Early and decisive actions to secure the financial and business fundamentals lay the foundation for future success. However, it is only by exploiting offensive strategies that companies can thrive in a low-growth, highly competitive economy. These strategies include the following:

1. Focus on innovation.
2. Capitalize on changes in the external environment.
3. Unleash marketing and advertising power.
4. Take the fight to your competitors.

5. Invest in the future through M&A and divestments.
6. Employ game-changing strategies.

■ FOCUS ON INNOVATION ■

History has shown us that innovation is the engine that spurs new periods of growth. We have already referred to Kondratiev's work and how some of the greatest technological advances heralded new eras of prosperity. And even if one does not subscribe to the theory of K-cycles, one need only look at the Great Depression to see how innovation can make all the difference to the fortunes of individual companies.

Take a look, for example, at IBM—a company that during the Great Depression did an effective job of combining research and development, investing in building technical capabilities, and understanding changing customer needs and business conditions. The small but growing business-machines industry was one of the worst affected during the Great Depression—the production of business machines saw a 60 percent decline between 1929 and 1932. Many firms filed for bankruptcy, and the few survivors scaled back costs.

IBM, then a relatively small player in the industry, was less severely affected than its larger rivals. It decided that it could leverage its position by maintaining (rather than reducing) production capacity and by increasing its investment in innovation.

These bold decisions were driven by Thomas J. Watson's conviction that the industry faced a huge opportunity for growth in the years ahead. In 1929, only 5 percent of business accounting functions were automated. Watson, then president of IBM, believed that the increasing complexity of business functions would eventually make the business machine indispensable. He also recognized that Depression-hit companies seeking to realize cost savings would turn to automation.

So, as demand began to fall in late 1929 and competitors cut back, IBM decided to accelerate the development of a state-of-the-art alphabetical accounting machine so that it could be ready for launch in early 1930. When the product hit the market, interest was strong—but sales were limited by the machine's high price point. IBM adjusted quickly by introducing a smaller, less expensive model in 1931. The new model appealed to existing customers (who had become very cost-conscious) and enabled IBM to attract new customers—particularly companies that had been unable to afford the company's larger machines. IBM also leveraged its product-leasing program to attract cost-conscious customers. By leasing its accounting machines instead of just selling them, IBM attracted companies that did not have sufficient capital to purchase its machines outright.

Starting in 1932, IBM committed 6 percent of its revenue to R&D. In order to make its investment as effective as possible, IBM created a corporate research laboratory—the first of its kind—that became a model for other firms to follow. It built the new laboratory next to its main manufacturing center in Endicott, New York. All its engineers were located there, under one roof, to facilitate the exchange of ideas within the R&D team and between the R&D and manufacturing teams. The mandate given to the research and engineering team was to focus on practical product needs rather than on pure research.

The investment and the process paid off—during the 1930s, IBM launched three times as many products as it had in the previous decade.

It was, however, in the second half of the decade that Watson's business acumen and insight into the potential of business machines proved to be unusually prescient and IBM's revenue growth really took off. As part of the New Deal, announced in 1933, many large-scale government projects started up. These projects created demand for sophisticated business machines that could keep track of the spending of significant amounts of public funds. IBM's innovative products were ready at the right moment and enabled the company to win many lucrative government contracts.

Throughout the decade, as demand and revenue increased, Watson kept IBM's factories open and humming and the workforce intact. He ordered the stockpiling of inventories when demand fell, convinced of the indispensable role of his business machines. (Between 1929 and 1932, IBM increased production capacity by a third.) Watson also retained the best talent by offering a range of benefits. According to the company's Web site, "IBM was among the first companies to provide group life insurance (1934), survivor benefits (1935), and paid vacations (1937)."

The decisions IBM made in the 1930s gave it a decisive and long-lasting advantage over its competitors. Its revenues doubled between 1928 and 1938, whereas industry revenues overall fell by 2 percent. Between 1928 and 1938, IBM leapfrogged from a distant fourth place to a close second, behind the now virtually forgotten Remington Rand.

It leveraged its relative financial strength to increase capacity and improve its technical capabilities just when others were cutting back. After the oil shocks of 1974 and during Japan's Lost Decade, many companies found success by following a similar strategy.

And this approach is just as relevant today.

Invest in R&D and Accelerate Product Development

During the Great Depression, R&D spending dropped significantly. But we find a consistent pattern in our research: companies like IBM that were able to sustain investment in R&D created enduring advantage. It is also true that downturn investments are often of better value, with less competition for scarce resources not only keeping costs down but also increasing availability. Playing catch-up with a company that continues to invest through difficult times is extremely difficult.

In the years before the Great Depression, the U.S. chemical industry had experienced a period of innovation and success. Much of that success continued through the 1930s, with the industry still remaining profitable despite a sharp drop in revenues. However, DuPont significantly outperformed the industry. The company's profits increased by 60 percent between 1929 and 1937, with its share of the profits of the chemical industry increasing from 20 percent to 32 percent over the same period. Rather than follow convention and cut back R&D in response to the Great Depression, DuPont expanded, recognizing that increasing investment in R&D could open up an innovation gap over its competitors. It adopted a policy of cost "refinement, not retrenchment," assessing research on the basis of its potential to deliver marketable products in a short time frame.[1] This practical commitment to rapid development cycles and the prioritization of investment that can yield quick returns are features of many successful innovators in difficult economic times.

DuPont used the downturn as an opportunity to take a hard look at its research programs, eliminating those that had little chance of success and increasing R&D spending on others with greater potential. The struggling ammonia division, for example, was redirected in the 1930s toward the development of nylon. Cutting its R&D budget in only one year during the Great Depression, DuPont increased its annual spending by a total of 93 percent between 1930 and 1939. Investment in R&D led directly to DuPont's introduction of neoprene in 1931 and nylon in 1939, giving it a first-mover advantage with two products that proved to be hugely successful for decades to come.

R&D budgets were similarly squeezed during Japan's Lost Decade. Shin-Etsu, the specialty chemicals company, used its strong financial position to gain an early lead in a new technology during the 2001 downturn.

In late 2000, Chihiro Kanagawa, Shin-Etsu's CEO, saw signs that the semiconductor industry was moving toward the use of large wafers in its manufacturing process. The standard wafer size at the time was 200 millimeters, but recent research had shown that shifting to the larger 300-millimeter wafers could cut the cost of production substantially—the only caveat being that it required significant investment up-front in technology and manufacturing facilities.

Because the technology sector was hit hard in the 2000 downturn, Japanese wafer manufacturers were even more hesitant about investing in expensive new production capabilities. Kanagawa, however, was convinced about the long-term cost-saving potential of the larger wafers, and the company enjoyed the strong cash position necessary to make the upgrades. He foresaw the benefit of being the first mover in a technology that, he believed, would become the norm for the industry.

So he took a calculated risk by accelerating the company's investment in the development of the 300-milimeter silicon wafer—the first company to do so—and spent $700 million on production facilities for the new product. This gave Shin-Etsu a one-year head start over rivals that responded only after demand for the new product increased significantly. Shin-Etsu's early lead proved to be decisive. By closely tailoring production to the needs of the semiconductor industry, Shin-Etsu quickly gained share in the market for the new wafers. By 2004, it commanded a nearly 50 percent share of the fast-growing market and became the market leader.[2]

Nitto Denko, a manufacturer of chemical and electrical components, followed a comparably aggressive new-product development strategy during the 1990s. The company launched a series of new products between 1994 and 2003, increasing the share of revenues from new products from 28 percent to 46 percent.

The strategy had three pillars. First, Nitto Denko exploited its existing manufacturing capabilities to develop new products—such as leveraging the capabilities that had been deployed in the manufacture of insulating tape for cables for the purpose of making packing tape. Second, it adapted existing products to new applications and new customers. For example, it applied its experience in making protective film (used primarily to protect automobiles during shipping) to develop protective materials for other glass and metal products. Third, Nitto Denko sold its existing products into new markets. Having expanded its range of protective materials for manufactured products, it began selling the same products to silicon wafer manufacturers.

Nitto Denko found that this strategy had an added benefit. It was able to obtain detailed information about customers in these markets, which enabled it to expand into other niche products and discover lucrative adjacent markets.

Nitto Denko's success was built on its strategy of entering or creating niche markets of approximately $10 million and aiming to become the top player in each market. In order to develop leadership within each niche market, the company chose to nest R&D facilities within individual business units, giving the units free rein over new-product development. In 1994, the company had 16 business units, each of which had R&D, manufacturing, and sales capabilities.

For Shin-Etsu Chemical and Nitto Denko—as for IBM and DuPont before them—the courage to invest heavily in innovation got them through the hard times and positioned them strongly for the period that followed.

■ CAPITALIZE ON CHANGES IN ■
THE EXTERNAL ENVIRONMENT

Like today's Great Recession, the three previous periods of recession that we studied were times when there were secular shifts in government policy, consumer behavior, risk appetites, and industry composition. Many of the most successful companies recognized these shifts early and either tailored their business models or developed and adapted their products to capitalize on the opportunities such changes present. They provide a good role model for today's companies.

Take Advantage of Changing Customer Behaviors or Attitudes

During the Great Depression, the emergence of scientific market-research methods profoundly deepened the consumer goods industry's understanding of the way consumers used and perceived its products. Procter & Gamble, for example, introduced synthetic detergents to the market, and—although technical breakthroughs played an important role—many of its product developments were informed by the market research techniques that P&G pioneered during those years.

In 1930, for example, P&G enlisted college-educated women to go door-to-door and conduct surveys of members of the company's core market—homemakers—about their views on household products. This and other research practices proved so useful that P&G more than quadrupled the budget of its market research department between 1930 and 1942—despite the difficult times.

Today, the use of these market research techniques is commonplace. However, it is rare that—when the economy falters—companies continue to invest in such techniques as heavily as P&G did during the Great Depression. Indeed, just as many managers will quickly trim their R&D spending, so will they just as quickly take the knife to the market research budget. But a lack of consumer understanding—especially when those very consumers are undergoing major shifts in preferences—can put a company at a serious disadvantage to competitors that continue to robustly develop new products based on changing customer needs and behaviors.

The Huggies brand launched by Kimberly-Clark in 1977—a period of double-digit inflation—was developed after completion of a major study on consumer preferences. This resulted in a dramatically new diaper design that more closely matched the shape of babies, employed new elastic materials, used tapes that could be refastened, and provided extra absorbency. The higher manufacturing costs associated with the new design necessitated a 30 percent price premium over other diapers, a difficult prospect during those inflationary times. Despite that obstacle, however, the superior quality of Huggies led to quick growth in market share: starting from zero in 1977, market share increased to 7 percent in 1980 and to 18 percent in 1983; by 1985, Huggies was the number one selling brand. This is further proof that consumers will pay for an innovative product that genuinely meets their needs—and will pay a premium for it even when times are tough.

A deep understanding of how consumers are responding to a prolonged downturn can lead a company to go beyond new-product innovation and even make changes to its fundamental business model. Had Kimberly-Clark not continually monitored how its consumers thought and behaved, the Huggies brand probably would not have achieved the success that it did.

The benefits of adapting to changes in customer preferences can also be seen in Japan during the difficult years of the 1990s. During the Lost Decade, Japan's retailing model moved toward discounters and mass merchants. Cash-strapped consumers had begun to buy a larger share of the products they needed from these outlets, and they also were steadily shifting toward the purchase of the private-label brands the mass merchants offered.

Seven-Eleven Japan, the country's largest chain of convenience stores, whose owner also controls the U.S. 7-Eleven stores, was already well positioned to benefit from these trends. Adapting to new demands, it aggressively invested in the development of private-label products. Collaborating with U.S. manufacturers, Seven-Eleven developed a private-label cola for the Japanese market that retailed at 25 percent less than the national brands, and a private-label beer that sold for 20 percent less. The company also leveraged the influence it wielded in the retail sector to convince suppliers to work with it to develop higher-margin private-label products. The manufacturers, afraid of losing shelf space to their competitors if they did not cooperate, reluctantly agreed. As a result of these moves, Seven-

Eleven continued to gain share and cemented its place as the market leader in one of the few industries that saw consistent revenue growth during the decade.

Asahi Breweries, a Japanese beer manufacturer, also rode the consumer trend toward bulk purchase of discounted products. As a late entrant to the industry, Asahi recognized that it would have little chance of growing fast if it chose to sell its products through traditional sales channels such as liquor stores, which were dominated by its major competitors. Instead, Asahi targeted discount chains and mass merchants. Although these outlets commanded a small share of the market in the early 1990s, Asahi believed that their influence was likely to increase. And competition for shelf space in these retailers was less intense.

Asahi's foresight enabled it to grow more quickly than it could have through the traditional channels, and its rise was helped by its major competitors' slow recognition of the growing influence of discounters. In fact, one major competitor finally shifted its focus toward discounters only in 1996, after it had already conceded a sizable share of the new and growing business to Asahi. Asahi's well-timed move played an important role in its success during the 1990s and eventually helped it to achieve market leadership.

This shift to private-label products continues today. In Europe, discounters such as Lidl and Aldi are gaining market share, and other retailers are aggressively increasing shelf space for private-label products. Manufacturers have started responding by strengthening the lower end of their product range.

Make the Most of Government Intervention

Some of the best opportunities that existed in the 1930s were those presented by the increasing role of government—and both GE and IBM were able to take advantage of them, as we will discuss in more detail.

While the global economy is not quite as weak today as it was in 1932, government programs will play an important role in reviving the economy over the next few years. This will present a sizable opportunity for many companies. The scale of these opportunities is even larger today than it was during the Great Depression; the first round of stimulus measures, which began in the third quarter of 2008, has amounted to more than $2 trillion, and there may be more rounds to come.

Governments today also account for a larger share of the economy. At the start of the Great Depression, the U.S. government's share of gross domestic product was below 10 percent. This share rose to 15 percent during the 1930s. In 2008, the U.S. government's share of GDP was already close to 20 percent; this share no doubt will rise over the next few years.

Today's stimulus measures have directly addressed a range of industries, including health care, infrastructure, clean technology, and education. More important, the impact of these measures will be felt beyond the industries that will receive the stimulus funds. The stimulus also will lead to second-order demand in complementary industries.

Two of the strongest companies of the last several decades—GE and IBM—were both beneficiaries of the opportunities created by New Deal programs during the Great Depression. Prior to the Depression, the Hoover administration had maintained a policy of limited government intervention in the economy. In 1932, however, Franklin D. Roosevelt was elected—along with a Democratic majority in Congress—on a platform of economic recovery through active government intervention. During the 1930s, the Roosevelt administration abandoned its objective of balanced budgets and launched what was then the largest stimulus plan in history—equivalent to around $500 billion today. However, relative to the size of the economy, the New Deal stimulus expenditure was enormous: over a three-year period, it averaged around 16.5 percent of U.S. GDP.

Initiatives such as the highway expansion program and the rural electrification program resulted in large contracts for a handful of private companies that had anticipated these opportunities. The early efforts of these companies to understand the commercial implications of such programs gave them a decisive advantage over their competitors. Indeed, so important was this flow of spending that some Great Depression companies became adept at lobbying government figures in order to influence spending allocations.

GE saw the potential of government contracts early on. Starting in 1931, Gerard Swope, GE's president, became an active public campaigner for Keynesian government-spending policies. GE capitalized on government spending across a range of new federal programs. The Tennessee Valley Authority, designed to provide economic development to the largely poor and rural American South, began the construction of dams across the Southeast. Construction of new electricity infrastructure, in turn, provided a large market for GE's electricity generation and transmission products.

GE also benefited from second-order effects of the rural electrification program. At the start of the 1930s, only 10 percent of rural households in the United States had electricity. By the end of the decade, this figure had jumped to 90 percent. During that period, not surprisingly, demand for consumer durable goods—especially those powered by the newly available electricity—increased rapidly. In the early 1930s, GE had started reorienting its portfolio away from capital goods, which was a declining market, toward the growing consumer-goods market. Since it understood the potential of the rural electrification program and saw its effects, GE accelerated its development of consumer goods. The company released the electric washing machine in 1930, and followed it up with food mixers, vacuum cleaners, and air conditioners throughout the 1930s. To help consumers purchase these products, GE launched the General Electric Credit Corporation in 1932 to provide credit to consumers unable to obtain financing from the highly constrained banks—just as IBM had done for industrial companies that wanted to buy its pricey business machines.

As we have seen, IBM also benefited from second-order effects of the New Deal—the demand for sophisticated accounting tools. In fact, IBM won the biggest contract of the New Deal era with the Social Security Administration (SSA) in 1935. The SSA needed to manage 120 million postings per year from 27 million claimants, so the contract proved very profitable for IBM—not only in terms of machine rentals but also in terms of the sale of the paper punch cards that the machines used in the days before the invention of internal memory. Thanks to this and other such government contracts, IBM's sales revenue grew by an average of 16 percent per year from 1935 until 1940.

GE and IBM were quick to recognize the potential of government contracts and put themselves in a position to benefit from them. Today, most companies have yet to take full account of the government's role in their plans—but some have clearly spotted the opportunities.

For example, Peter Löscher, the CEO of Siemens, was reported by the *Financial Times* as believing that "infrastructure programs launched worldwide and the push for a green modernization would spur growth in the industrial sector."[3] He said that Siemens fully intended to take advantage of the opportunities. The majority (56 percent) of the company executives we surveyed in September 2009 also share this view.

These opportunities are not limited to fiscal stimuli. Companies would be well advised to look more broadly at the way governments are shifting their industrial policies. Better still, they should endeavor to influence the formulation of such policies.

Either way, it would be well worth the effort to scout for these opportunities in a proactive way. And it would be well worth remembering that the government tap will not be turned on forever. As U.S. Treasury Secretary Henry Morgenthau stated in 1939, "We have tried spending money. We are spending more than we have ever spent before, and it does not work. . . . I say after eight years of this Administration we have just as much unemployment as when we started, and an enormous debt to boot!"[4]

■ UNLEASH ADVERTISING AND MARKETING POWER ■

Advertising and marketing budgets, classified as discretionary spending, are usually the first to get the ax during any recession—because, even more than R&D, their immediate contribution to the top line is hard to ascertain. Given this natural reflex for most companies, advertising costs tend to fall dramatically during downturns. Between 1929 and 1932, U.S. advertising expenditures fell by 29 percent in real terms.

There is a similar knee-jerk reaction today. But the irony is that because so many companies cut their spending during a recession, the cost of advertising actually drops significantly, and the few firms that continue to advertise aggressively capture a larger share of voice at relatively favorable rates.

This increased prominence at relatively low cost can become a powerful tool, as P&G found during the Great Depression. Although the consumer goods industry had suffered less than other industries during that time, companies were still aggressively cutting back their advertising budgets. Seeing an opportunity to reach its core customers (then referred to as "housewives") by advertising on radio, the company launched the first daytime serial radio program in 1933. P&G advertised its core product—soap—on these programs. They soon became known as "soap operas."

So successful was the first program that P&G was encouraged to launch more, and by the end of the 1930s, P&G had established itself as one of the biggest advertisers on radio. Between 1935 and 1937, P&G doubled its spending on radio advertising and then doubled it again from 1937 to 1939. Meanwhile, overall spending on marketing in the United States remained nearly flat.

It is not just the big companies that can exploit the benefits of advertising during a downturn in order to build visibility and brand recognition more cheaply than during an upturn. As in the Great Depression, today's environment creates an especially valuable opportunity for innovative companies whose business model is geared toward the lower end of the market. Part of Chrysler's success, for example, can be attributed to the heavy publicity and marketing tactics it employed in the early 1930s to popularize the new Plymouth.

In 1931, Chrysler launched a reengineered Plymouth model with a unique new engine-mounting system that eliminated a vibration and noise design problem. This new feature was dubbed "floating power," and the launch of the new Plymouth PA model was accompanied by an advertising campaign that focused on its superior technology. Print advertisements were run with the slogan "Smoothness of an eight, the economy of a four," highlighting Chrysler's selling point that it offered luxury at a discount price. Plymouth also used racing as an inexpensive form of publicity, setting in 1931 the nonstop transcontinental speed record from San Francisco to New York and back. Sales for Chrysler's Plymouth line increased by 66 percent between 1930 and 1931.

Much of this marketing paid off in the years after the Great Depression, with Chrysler winning a reputation as one of the most innovative companies in the automobile industry. As consumer demand revived, Chrysler's unusual aerodynamic cars became increasingly popular. Having the courage not only to develop but also to promote these cars during the downturn created the platform for success when the economy turned.

A more recent example is Uniqlo, the Japanese apparel retailer, which combined new-product development with aggressive marketing during the late 1990s. At a time when the market was dominated by designer brands offering good-quality clothing at high prices, Uniqlo's primary focus on private-label casual wear was a differentiator. Most of its clothing was unisex, reasonably priced, and of good quality. By the mid-1990s, after 10 years in business, Uniqlo still was a relatively small player with just a 7 percent market share.

In 1998, the company launched an aggressive marketing campaign to publicize a new range of fleece jackets attractively priced at 1,900 yen ($14 at the time) and available in 13 colors. The 18 billion yen ($137 million) campaign was a rarity in an industry that, as a whole, typically spent less than half that amount. The jackets, which had been codeveloped with Toray Industries, a fiber and materials company, were the first range of fleece clothing to be introduced in Japan.

The campaign for the jackets was a huge success—Uniqlo sold 2 million units in the autumn/winter season in 1998. By 2000, it had sold 20 million jackets. Not only did the marketing campaign move a lot of fleece, but it also played a key role in establishing the Uniqlo brand. By the end of the decade, Uniqlo had become the market leader, increasing its market share from 7 percent to 23 percent, a dramatic increase relative to the growth of Japan's economy at the time.

The Uniqlo story offers three lessons. First, consumers are happy to buy appealing new products even when times are tough—especially if they are well priced. Second, the money invested in the development and promotion of new products is money well spent. Third, achieving a high share of voice—even an overwhelming share of voice—comes at a lower cost in straitened times. At best, catching up when the economic tide turns comes at a disproportionately high cost; at worst, it is impossible.

■ TAKE THE FIGHT TO YOUR COMPETITORS ■

Competition intensifies during a recession as markets contract, and companies are left with an excess capacity of workers, facilities, and products. In the new era of slow growth, companies will do everything they can to protect—and grow—their share of the market. To do this, they will expand into new geographic regions, enter new product and service categories, and reach out to different groups of customers. This means that companies will have to expect new rivals to come from many places—including not only other countries but also other industries.

Companies based in the rapidly developing economies—notably China and India—were already presenting traditional multinational companies with serious competition prior to the downturn. This is likely to increase in the coming years. The rapidly developing economies have experienced milder downturns than those in the developed world—and are emerging stronger than ever. This will benefit their companies.

Companies in the technology sector will also face competition from unexpected quarters as hardware and software manufacturers venture into each other's traditional territories. Cisco has been aggressively expanding beyond its core market of network components, entering more than 30 "market adjacencies" such as virtual health care, consumer electronics, and teleconferencing. Cisco sees the downturn as a clear opportunity to go on the offensive with a diversification strategy.

In such an environment, companies cannot rely solely on defensive strategies—it is essential that they take the fight to their competitors. To do so, some companies leverage their existing strengths, while others reinvent themselves with game-changing strategies, as we'll see.

The Fight in Japan in the 1990s

During the Lost Decade, slow growth and intermittent deflation exerted downward pressure on revenues for many industries in Japan. Volumes in the Japanese beer market, for example, were virtually stagnant between 1990 and 2003. This also was a period of significant churn within the industry. By the end of the 1990s, Asahi had displaced the market leader (which once held a 50 percent share).

Asahi's success was not entirely the result of its focus on distribution through discount and mass-market channels; it also challenged its competitors with an aggressive "replacement program."

In 1997, the beer industry came to an agreement that the "use by" date marked on its beer products would be nine months from the date of production. Very shortly after the agreement was made, Asahi announced that it would initiate a "replacement program" so that all its products would have use-by dates of three months or less. Then it launched an advertising campaign emphasizing the greater freshness of Asahi beer.

Asahi's competitors, caught flat-footed, felt compelled to respond by updating inventories with newer products at higher costs. But Asahi had been careful to build up its supply of three-month products (and reduce its inventory of nine-month products) so that it did not actually have to replace any inventory at all.

Asahi was not afraid to take on its competitors. The company also launched a campaign in 1993 promoting itself as the "No. 1 non-heat-treated beer" to associate itself with the number one image. By 1996, in the face of changing public demand driven by Asahi's clever positioning, even the market leader had responded, switching its own process to a non-heat-treated one. This strategy backfired for the market leader because the change altered the taste of its premium lager and resulted in a drop-off in demand.

A similar example can be found in the Japanese consumer-electronics industry. During the 1990s, Yamada Denki, a mid-size consumer electronics retailer, chose to compete directly with market leader Kojima to gain share. After choosing to locate its stores next door to Kojima, Yamada launched a campaign advertising itself as the number one low-cost retailer and guaranteeing the lowest price on every product. In fact, it promised customers a 3 percent discount on the price if they found a competitor offering a lower price on the same product.

The strategy, which leveraged Yamada's state-of-the-art consumer-information and inventory-management system to stock the widest and most popular range of products, proved to be extremely successful. Although Yamada earned a lower margin on its products, its selling, general, and administrative expenses were lower than those of its competitors. Using its cost advantage to keep prices low, Yamada maximized volumes and rapidly gained share over Kojima. In 2000, Yamada leapfrogged into second place, and by 2001, it had become the market leader.

While Asahi and Yamada Denki were smaller players that competed aggressively to become market leaders, Seven-Eleven Japan competed aggressively to cement its position as market leader in the convenience store sector during the 1990s. It began the Lost Decade as a market leader, but it was not complacent about its privileged position. Between 1990 and 1999, the company doubled its 4,000-store network to 8,000, giving it a considerable advantage over both its competitors and its suppliers.

Seven-Eleven leveraged its market leadership and brand recognition to partner with Japan's major food manufacturers in developing cobranded products that would be retailed exclusively at Seven-Eleven. Unlike private-label products that sold at a low price point, these cobranded products could be sold at a price equal to that of branded products—a new idea for convenience stores. Seven-Eleven, which had developed a good understanding of customer needs and was able to apply that knowledge to the development of cobranded products, realized an increase in margins over its discount private-label products. Of course, this meant a lower margin for Seven-Eleven's partners, but they did not complain because they gained an exclusive access to Seven-Eleven that resulted in increased sales volume for them.

One well-known example of Seven-Eleven's codevelopment process was ice cream products. In 1994, it worked with five major food companies, including Morinaga and Yukijirushi. They held "ice cream workshops" twice a month to discuss new-product ideas. These sessions resulted in the creation of a range of cobranded products that replaced half the ice cream products that had previously lined the shelves at Seven-Eleven. In 2000, Seven-Eleven partnered with Nissin, the top instant-noodle manufacturer, to codevelop a line of new products and branded them with the names of famous noodle restaurants. This product line, which sold exclusively at Seven-Eleven, was extremely successful and achieved five times more sales than national brands.

Beyond the codevelopment of products, cobranding also improved inventory management. Seven-Eleven provided daily order and inventory data to manufacturers—an unprecedented level of information-sharing at the time. This allowed the manufacturers to adjust their supply quickly in response to demand shifts.

Seven-Eleven's wide reach and ability to negotiate exclusive deals made codevelopment an attractive choice for Japan's top manufacturers. Other retailers such as Lawson and Family Mart adopted a similar private-label and cobranding strategy, especially after seeing the success of Seven-Eleven's private-label ice cream products. However, being smaller in size, and therefore less attractive to manufacturers, they were less successful.

The Fight in the United States in the Aftermath of the Oil Shock

McDonald's took the fight to its competitors, particularly Burger King, during the U.S. oil crisis and recession of the

1970s by accelerating the pace at which it opened new stores. Prior to 1973, McDonald's had opened about 300 stores annually, but starting in that year, the company went into overdrive. It opened 445 stores in 1973, 515 stores in 1974, and 474 in 1975. Although Burger King had been matching or surpassing McDonald's rate of new-store openings in the late 1960s, it subsequently slowed to less than 200 new restaurants per year largely owing to the caution of its new owner, Pillsbury.

Although Burger King did its best to catch up to McDonald's at the end of the decade, McDonald's was too far ahead. Jim McLamore, the cofounder of Burger King, believes that the slowing of Burger King's expansion in the 1970s was a key reason why McDonald's held a 2.2 to 1 lead over Burger King in U.S. hamburger sales by the 1990s.[5] The Burger King example shows the risk of choosing not to respond forcefully to the challenge posed by a core competitor even when economic times are tough—and the reward that comes from taking the fight to your competitors.

Contrast this with the response of Kimberly-Clark in the personal hygiene market. In 1971, Johnson & Johnson was the first company to introduce a new "tabless" sanitary pad. The superior design became very popular with consumers. Recognizing the threat early on, Kimberly-Clark responded with its own tabless product within six months. While it lost market share to Johnson & Johnson in those six months, its quick response helped to limit the erosion it suffered in market share.

The decisive tactics used by these companies were important in allowing them to carve out a larger share of the slow-growing pie. Perhaps the lesson most worth remembering is that such tactics—the unleashing of disproportionate force or attacking the heart of a competitor's profitability—become more damaging when deployed in a low-growth environment. Companies that stick with tradition and deploy solely defensive strategies risk losing out.

■ INVEST IN THE FUTURE THROUGH OPPORTUNISTIC ■ M&A AND STRATEGIC DIVESTMENTS

One of the most formidable weapons that companies can use is the restructuring of the corporate portfolio—either growing it through mergers and acquisitions (M&A) or pruning it through strategic divestments.

Conduct Opportunistic M&A

Often, the most effective strategy to achieve growth in a sluggish industry is to acquire weaker competitors. While this is easier said than done, M&A activity can become more effective during a recession when premiums are lower and opportunities are richer. Downturns can present unique and inexpensive opportunities to acquire rivals that find themselves credit constrained. A study conducted by The Boston Consulting Group reveals that, on average, deals completed during downturns outperform those completed during upturns by 14 percentage points on the basis of relative total shareholder return.

Gannett Company used such a strategy to gain scale during the recession in the United States in the 1970s. The recession had delivered a twin blow to the newspaper industry—squeezing revenues while causing costs to rise rapidly. Gannett used the opportunity to acquire small local newspaper chains that were on the verge of bankruptcy. Through the acquisitions, the company gained a significant economy of scale in reporting and advertising. Between 1970 and 1980, Gannett's earnings before interest and taxes (EBIT) margin grew from 16 percent to 25 percent, and in 1980, it had the highest EBIT margin among its three major national competitors.

P&G and IBM successfully conducted M&A during the Great Depression to quickly diversify their product portfolios through the purchase of companies that had complementary brands and technologies. To expand its leadership in the U.S. soap market, P&G acquired 12 brands during the 1920s and was preparing to purchase others when the Depression struck. Rather than abandon its expansion plans, P&G went ahead with the acquisition of James S. Kirk & Co. in June 1930. The same year, it entered the U.K. and French soap markets with the acquisition of, respectively, Fairy and Monsavon. Its fourth soap-brand acquisition of the era occurred in 1937 with the purchase of Monogen in Japan. Counting its own brands as well as those it acquired, P&G introduced more successful products during the 1930s than it had during the previous decade or would in the subsequent one.

DuPont followed a less common strategy of opportunistic M&A. In 1930, with many suppliers failing, the company was threatened with a shortage of raw materials. It just so happened that one of the suppliers facing bankruptcy was Roessler & Hasslacher Chemical. DuPont made a quick move to acquire Roessler & Hasslacher—an acquisition that helped DuPont not only to secure the crucial inputs it needed for its own products but also to gain entry into the electrochemical market through a range of specialized chemicals that eventually were used in electroplating, refrigeration, bleaching, disinfectants, and insecticides.

Make Strategic Divestments

The decision to divest a business is always a difficult one. However, divestments can become an important source of capital when resources are limited, allowing companies to refocus and strengthen their core business.

BCG research indicates that companies divesting assets enjoy substantial gains, increasing shareholder value by 1.5 percentage points across all economic cycles. In fact, the study finds that the capital market reaction is even more positive during downturns than during upturns. Although the seller's immediate concern is to obtain the best possible price for the asset, the additional increase in shareholder value achieved though the divestment often outweighs any loss incurred in the sale. More important, divestment decisions that are made early in a recession help the seller to obtain a higher price for the asset and also put the company in a relatively better position to go on the offensive.

Chihiro Kanagawa, CEO of Shin-Etsu, took over leadership of the specialty chemicals company in early 1990, at the beginning of the Lost Decade in Japan. As noted in the previous chapter, one of Kanagawa's earliest decisions was to divest Shin-Etsu's noncore financial business and focus on the core polyvinyl chloride market. The divesture gave Shin-Etsu an early advantage and allowed it to enter the recession leaner than many of its competitors. Indeed, Shin-Etsu was ahead of the curve as the trend in Japan toward greater diversification of companies continued throughout the 1990s. Research now has shown a negative relationship between diversification and business performance in Japan during the 1990s, a fact that many companies finally realized by the early 2000s when a wave of divestments swept across Japanese businesses.[6]

Divestments were also crucial to Walgreens' turnaround during the 1970s recession in the United States. During the 1960s and early 1970s, Walgreens had acquired and launched three restaurant chains, a department store chain, and a chain of optical shops. None of these acquisitions fitted within Walgreens' core drugstore business. In 1977, the new CEO, Charles R. Walgreen III, made the decision to divest all the company's noncore divisions. Over the course of 11 years, Walgreens divested seven substantial divisions. The divestment helped to free limited resources, allowing the company to strengthen its drug retailing business and return to profitability.

During the same period, Kimberly-Clark used the capital raised from the divestment of its underperforming coated-paper business to invest in R&D for its consumer products. This investment resulted in the development of its successful Huggies diaper brand and provided the necessary capital to aggressively advertise and market this new brand.

Throughout much of Japan's Lost Decade, Takeda, the market-leading pharmaceutical company, maintained its highly diversified conglomerate structure—a strategy typical of many Japanese companies. While pharmaceuticals were its core business, Takeda maintained joint ventures in veterinary drugs, vitamins, food products, agricultural products, chemicals, and resins.

With its relentless focus on reducing costs, Takeda managed to improve its position relative to its competitors. But in 2002, Takeda's leadership decided to take more drastic action. CEO Kunio Takeda, recognizing that Takeda's pharmaceutical business accounted for 80 percent of revenues and achieved the highest profits, decided to divest its other businesses. This was no easy move because the company controlled between 34 and 49 percent of each of the joint ventures across its six product categories. It was also an unusual move because diversification was the norm in the Japanese pharmaceutical industry, and under-performing units were often subsidized by profitable ones. The move paid off for Takeda, however. From 2002 to 2003, its margins increased by 2.5 percent, and EBIT increased by 29 percent.

These examples highlight the importance of a good divestment strategy. At a time when most companies should be examining their business portfolios, looking for potential divestments, most are not. In our survey of company executives, only 44 percent of respondents said they had taken divestment-related action in 2009. Fewer still said they were planning such actions in 2010. In contrast, some 73 percent of companies were planning to increase M&A activity in 2010.

■ EMPLOY GAME-CHANGING STRATEGIES ■

The damaged economy opens up some opportunities for game-changing strategies. True game-changing strategies are, in essence, forms of fundamental business model innovation. They may well draw on many individual elements of the strategies we have already discussed, but what distinguishes business model innovation is the number of strategic pieces being changed.

For companies that respond not just by changing a single component but by changing much or all of their business system, the Great Recession and the following slow-growth period can be a watershed. BCG analysis shows that business model innovation provides greater returns over the short and long term when compared with individual process, product, or service innovations. After three years, companies completing successful business model innovation were found, on average, to have delivered a total shareholder return premium of 8.5 percentage points over their industry rivals and 6.8 percentage points over those companies completing simple process or product innovation. After five years, the premium was 6 percentage points. In a difficult, competitive environment, such an advantage is very significant.

There are many examples of business model innovation, some of which are even more naturally suited to the current times than they were to previous downturns. Let us now describe some of these innovations.

Adopt a Low-Cost Business Model

With customers trading down and businesses cutting back, now could be the right time to develop a low-cost business model. Aside from any potential to achieve greater sales volumes on the back of lower prices, low-cost business models promote management discipline and unambiguous value propositions for customers and can even generate customer loyalty. Low-cost business models can work in good economic times or in tough ones, but launching such a model when growth is slow can protect margins or allow for much more competitive pricing.

There are four essential elements to operating a typical low-cost business model:

1. *Relentlessly pursue the lowest possible price.* Eliminate all noncritical features, and do not maintain costly loyalty programs.
2. *Focus on cost savings in all areas except for advertising and marketing.* (And even then, smart procurement can reduce the effective cost.) Developing permanent and revolving cost-cutting routines is helpful, and price should be central to the advertising and marketing message.

3. *Devote attention to delivering the basics.* Low prices should not mean low value but rather an alignment of price and value.

4. *Make flexibility and a broad job definition the norm.* In low-cost airlines, for example, flight attendants also clean the cabins between flights.

Take a look at steelmaker Nucor. In the 1970s and 1980s, it showed that a low-cost model can be used to take on a wide range of competitors. In the mid-1970s, Nucor was a minimill steel company like many others. It used the same equipment (the highly efficient electric arc furnace), used recycled steel products for its raw material inputs, made simple and inexpensive steel parts, and had few manufacturing plants.

In the second half of the 1970s, Nucor developed a national chain of plants that all produced the same low-end steel products and that were placed in equally spaced locations across the country in order to reduce transportation time and costs. Simultaneously, Nucor used a decentralized management structure and had a nonunionized workforce. That business model—which today would be known as a low-cost model—was quickly successful relative to other minimill companies that lacked Nucor's scale.

After succeeding in the minimill market, Nucor proceeded to use its business model to compete directly with the large, integrated steel mills that produced high-value products but were encumbered by a large cost base. In the 1980s, Nucor gradually moved up the value chain, taking on the integrated mills across many product categories. All the while, Nucor focused on large product runs and resisted the temptation to offer the same kind of customized products as its integrated mill competitors. As companies strove to reduce their cost base in the inflationary environment of the late 1970s and early 1980s, Nucor's lower prices persuaded customers to abandon their long-standing relationships with integrated U.S. steelmakers.

Shift from Selling Products to Selling Services or Outcomes

Another way to transform a company in a low-growth economy is to shift from the sale of products to the offering of services or outcomes. Rather than buying the product and obtaining a service from it, this model turns the equation on its head by using the product to sell either a service or a specific outcome. IBM in the Great Depression and Cessna Aircraft in the downturn of the early 1980s are good examples of companies that transformed themselves in this way.

IBM's offer to rent accounting machines rather than selling them was very successful because it reduced the up-front capital expenditure for companies. Accounting machines were popular because they improved efficiency and reduced costs for companies—but they were costly to purchase outright. Renting the machines also enabled IBM to lock in more customers to whom it could sell its high-margin paper punch cards—a pricing mechanism with which users of modern printer cartridges are all too familiar. But in order to make this service business work, IBM had to develop a completely different cash-flow equation, a different pricing and sales process, and a different approach to residual value and inventory management.

In the early 1980s, when Cessna's business jet division was heavily affected by the economic downturn, it launched a new business-jet leasing program. By bundling jet leasing with the offer of hangar space, jet refueling, and pilots, Cessna improved its value proposition while reducing the risk and up-front capital expenditures for its customers. It also required Cessna to develop and manage a new set of capabilities.

In the Great Recession, some companies have been making the products-to-services move. For instance, in March 2009, Daikokuya, a Japanese luxury handbag retailer, launched a handbag rental service that allowed customers to rent expensive handbags for short periods of time. The company also developed a rent-to-own program, allowing customers to pay the difference between their rental costs and the price of the handbag if they decided to purchase it. By lowering the up-front cost of using a handbag, and by letting people try out a product, Daikokuya was able to attract new—and retain existing—customers who were feeling the economic pinch.

Deconstruction

Deconstruction is an approach that disassembles the value chain and then looks to develop a solution that can provide faster, lower-cost, and more reliable products and services. In essence, it involves outsourcing internal functions to more efficient providers.

This business model innovation can take three forms:

1. *Shared development* lowers capital intensity and shares product risk across a range of suppliers.
2. *Orchestration* leverages a network of suppliers, providing more flexibility and lower costs while often offering a superior product.
3. *Facilitation* connects the buyers of products directly with a range of suppliers, allowing a company to facilitate rather than intermediate between buyers and suppliers.

RadioShack's substantial success in the 1970s was largely the result of its deconstructed model of product development and production. By working with Japanese electronics companies, RadioShack was able to develop and manufacture new private-label consumer electronics products.

To manufacture its products, RadioShack applied the orchestration method, using a wide range of electronics components suppliers while maintaining tight control of the process. In this way, it was able to minimize risk and, at the same time, develop more innovative and superior consumer electronics products at lower prices.

In 1973, RadioShack's EBIT margin was 7 percent, but that margin increased to 12 percent in 1975 following an expansion of its private-label electronic products range. This was a remarkable performance given the fact that the EBIT margin for the whole of the retail industry in 1975 was 7 percent.

New Businesses Can Thrive in a Downturn

As tough as the Great Depression was, companies were still created, and smaller companies were able to grow quickly, as demonstrated by Chrysler. Revlon, another household name today, was started in 1932, the worst year of the Great Depression. More recently, in the 1970s, FedEx was founded and Wal-Mart grew quickly—not *despite* but *because* of tough economic conditions. While high inflation and low economic growth presented serious challenges for other businesses, the forms of business model innovation adopted by FedEx and Wal-Mart allowed them to capitalize on those trends.

When Federal Express (as it was then called) started operating in 1973, it offered a new model of business with an entirely new product—an airline dedicated to freight that could deliver overnight. At the time, the fastest air delivery service in the United States took two days to deliver packages, shipping them from point to point through the domestic airline network.

Federal Express completely changed that. By obtaining its own fleet of small jets and routing them through a hub and spoke system, the company was able to guarantee overnight delivery. All packages, regardless of where they originated, were flown to the hub in Memphis, sorted overnight, and then flown onward to their destinations in the early morning.

The early 1970s were an inauspicious time to launch a company. Six months after Federal Express began operations, the oil shock hit. With the United States facing oil shortages, the price of fuel quadrupled over the subsequent months. While this was clearly a challenge for a company like Federal Express that relied so heavily on jet fuel, the company's management also saw an opportunity in the crisis.

As U.S. businesses were hit hard, corporate executives cut back on the use of corporate jets, resulting in a surplus of used business jets. That surplus led to a sharp drop in prices, and Federal Express moved quickly to buy the jets. Federal Express' opportunistic capital spending allowed it to expand its capacity rapidly so that between April 1973 and May 1974 it increased the size of its fleet from 6 to 25 jets. Such fast expansion provided Federal Express with greater economy of scale—and by 1976 it was already profitable.

For Wal-Mart, the 1970s also presented a growth opportunity. Founded in 1962, the U.S. retailer's growth had been gradual throughout the decade. From 1970, when it formally incorporated, growth was rapid—the number of stores grew at an average rate of 26 percent through the 1970s. Revenues also shot up in that decade, at no point more quickly than the period

1973–1977. In those years, revenues quadrupled. It is not a coincidence that in those years of spectacular growth for Wal-Mart, the U.S. economy experienced a recession and high inflation. Wal-Mart's low-cost business model innovation allowed it to accelerate when times were tough and customers were price sensitive.

As with any company that has a low-cost business model, Wal-Mart strove to reduce costs in every way possible. One area in which it achieved spectacular success was logistics, and it achieved cost savings by developing a different expansion strategy than other retailers. Competitors such as Kmart expanded their retail networks by opening new stores in different cities, stretching their centralized distribution networks over greater and greater distances.

Wal-Mart followed a different model. It first established a distribution center to serve a metropolitan area before opening any stores there. Once it had a distribution center in place, Wal-Mart rapidly expanded the number of stores in that area. It then repeated that model of development in other metropolitan areas, first expanding through the South and then across the whole of the United States.

Wal-Mart's model of localized distribution—together with cutting-edge computerized inventory-management software—led to substantial savings on fuel costs, especially as gasoline prices increased rapidly in the 1970s. Moreover, these logistics breakthroughs allowed the company to keep its costs down as inflation ramped up, and price-sensitive customers reacted positively. Between 1970 and 1977, Wal-Mart's revenue growth was 171 percent greater than that of competing discount retailer Kmart. In the Great Recession, Wal-Mart has once again performed extraordinarily well owing to its focus on low prices and the best distribution and logistics networks in the business.

Wal-Mart outperformed its rivals, recording EBIT growth of 7 percent in 2008 compared with the −5 percent average EBIT growth of its 10 main national competitors.

How Uniqlo Established a Successful Low-Priced Casual Wear Brand in Japan

Uniqlo, the Japanese casual apparel retailer, changed its business model in order to thrive in a competitive and uncertain environment. The Uniqlo brand, established in 1984, was originally positioned as a low-cost retailer of casual wear. Uniqlo's founder, Tadashi Yanai, believed that the dominance of designer and character brands would eventually falter and that casual wear would become more popular, just as it had in the United States. Inspired by the Gap and Limited chains, Yanai's aim was to create a brand with a similar universal appeal.

In the first half of the 1990s, Uniqlo's business model was focused on keeping prices low while supplying high-quality products. This goal was achieved through offshore production in China and Hong Kong and the adoption of low-cost warehouse-style store formats in inexpensive suburban areas. Management principles were borrowed primarily from the fast-food industry and resulted in substantial standardization.

All Uniqlo stores were laid out identically, and inventories were controlled though a central database. Store managers were given very little autonomy and were expected to consult the store manual on all aspects of day-to-day operations. The result was indeed a replication of the fast-food industry—an efficient and reliable supply chain of largely commoditized products.

This model proved to be successful. Store numbers increased from 29 in 1991 to 300 by 1997, and market share grew from 1 percent in 1991 to 7.3 percent by 1996.

Despite these successes, however, Uniqlo remained a peripheral player in the apparel retail market. Its presence and image were associated with the suburbs and small towns, which limited its ability to compete with the larger national chains.

Recognizing this constraint, Uniqlo's management made a series of key decisions in the late 1990s that propelled the company from a regional to a national stage and reshaped its image from a producer of standardized products to a retailer known for customer-focused innovation.

Until 1996, Uniqlo stores had stocked a mix of private-label and branded products. In 1997, management made the decision to stock only private-label products and to establish a clear brand focus. Simultaneously, company management reshaped Uniqlo's image, deciding to move from suburban to Main Street stores. This resulted in the opening of the first Uniqlo store in Tokyo's high-fashion Harajuku district in 1998. Meanwhile, the company discarded traditional advertising channels—such as door-to-door pamphlet distribution—in favor of TV and poster ads that promoted Uniqlo's new, trendier image.

The sales strategy shifted: instead of trying to sell as much as possible of what was produced, the company sought to develop blockbuster products that would sell out. This new focus resulted in the launch of its first range of fleece jackets in 1998—which we described earlier.

To make this strategy work, Uniqlo required changes in management style: store managers were given greater autonomy and incentivized to increase store sales. Uniqlo also rationalized its production system. By 1998, 90 percent of its merchandise was produced through contract manufacturing in China, which ensured low prices. It consolidated the number of factories, reducing the number from 140 to 40. It also set up an office in

Shanghai in 1999 to develop closer ties with its manufacturers and closely monitor product quality.

As a result, Uniqlo flourished. It increased its market share from 7.3 percent to 23.3 percent between 1997 and 2000 and became the market leader.

■ OF THE CREATIVE FORCES OF ■
DESTRUCTION AND LEADERSHIP

"This process of Creative Destruction is the essential fact about capitalism. It is what capitalism consists in and what every capitalist concern has got to live in."[7] So wrote Joseph Schumpeter.

For companies that have prospered during the Great Recession, a well-earned sense of accomplishment and relief may be in order. Executives have been forced to make tough decisions with wide-ranging and long-term implications. Getting through the downturn was no easy task. Unfortunately, the path will not become easier in the near future.

As Schumpeter pointed out more than a half century ago, the process of creative destruction in a capitalist system never ceases. Heightened exogenous stress—such as that caused by a recession—may accelerate the process of destruction, but creative destruction will persist even in the absence of shocks.

This process of creative destruction has two implications for companies today related to the current status of the damaged economy. First, companies that have been weakened by the recession or that have failed to adapt may yet succumb. Second, even if a company survives the downturn in good shape, the actions taken now will shape its pathway into the future.

BCG's analysis shows that those companies that outperformed in past recessions widened their lead for many years afterward, beating the subsequent cycles of creative destruction. This means that decisions made today could significantly shape the long-term future of a company. Of course, management is not as simple a process as identifying positive actions and executing them. It also takes talent and leadership. Many of the companies we have cited in this book were led by CEOs who were well known in their time—and some are still remembered today. The leaders of the successful companies in the Great Depression are particularly iconic: Alfred P. Sloan of GM, Thomas J. Watson of IBM, and Gerard Swope of GE. And that is no accident. Tough times call for brave and decisive leadership. Some of our winners took great gambles in building inventories, developing new products, or maintaining advertising spending and R&D. Many acted early to take firm action on the business and financial fundamentals—making the tough decisions about people and plants, not just about cutting executive travel or training events.

Those leaders also held strong, well-articulated visions for the future of their industries and companies. For Watson, it was a future in which accounting functions at companies large and small would be performed with IBM machines. For Swope, it was a future in which household life would be made progressively easier through the use of new GE products.

The choices made in the Great Depression turned those visions into reality. But they were not easy choices to make, nor were they easy to implement. Strong, effective leadership is essential for selecting the right set of actions, motivating an organization to execute them, and adjusting course when necessary. While the process of creative destruction may be inevitable, the precise outcomes are not.

Leadership, as we describe in the next and final chapter, really does make a difference.

CHAPTER 6

A NEW MANAGERIAL MIND-SET

The world has entered a tough period. As we have discussed, the era—sometimes dubbed the "new normal"—will be marked by slow growth and a set of new realities that result from the difficult economic climate.

Managing a company in this new era will feel altogether different from the way it has felt in prior years—and much will rest on how CEOs and management teams are willing to challenge their existing managerial mind-set.

One business leader in our survey compared this challenge to a hiking experience: "When I descended into the Grand Canyon, I was happy as I reached the bottom—but then I looked up, and I realized that getting back to the top was going to be an even bigger challenge. So now, while we can rejoice in the fact that the recession has ended, it looks like the long and painful way up has only just begun."

Over much of the last 20 years, it was possible (if not always achievable) to be successful simply by riding market growth. The challenge now is to be successful despite anemic markets and in the face of significantly intensified competition. For many executives, managing in a slow-growth environment—where the battle to gain market share is all-important—is a new phenomenon. It certainly changes the competitive rules of the game. And the task is not simply to seek growth for growth's sake. A dynamic corporate culture requires growth in order to offer talented people an opportunity for personal development and satisfying careers.

We have identified some of the strategies that companies should deploy to survive and thrive. Taken at face value, they may look like common sense. How can it ever be wrong to lower costs and increase revenues?

But we focus on these strategies because they have a proven history of working in recessionary times. What is more, these commonsense approaches are not as easy to implement as it might seem, especially in difficult times—and their successful execution requires decisive leadership and a willingness to think unconventionally.

Today, the margin for error for business leaders is smaller than it has been for a very long time. For a company to be successful, it is mandatory to achieve sustained differentiation. Companies that fail to do so will find that they have nowhere to hide.

Good strategies will stand out; poor ones will result in a weakened business model, which in turn will lead to a sustained and possibly irrecoverable loss of competitive position. As we have described throughout this book, empirical evidence from past recessions shows that companies that outperform during a downturn tend to accelerate ahead of their competition during the recovery. Moreover, the risk to market leaders is correspondingly higher when they are slow to respond during volatile times.

Of course, not all the new realities that we have described will appear at once or affect all companies and industries in the same way—and some may turn out to be temporary rather than permanent. But executives need to ready themselves for a journey on a road that could be long, winding, and steep.

It will therefore no longer be enough to play just to play; it will be necessary to play to win. As Vince Lombardi, legendary coach of the Green Bay Packers football team in the 1950s and 1960s, once put it, "Show me a good loser, and I'll show you a loser."

■ New Realities, New Managerial Mind-set ■

To cope with today's challenges, executives will be required to question, reassess, and redefine their managerial mind-set. They will need to reexamine the context in which they make decisions and act as leaders. Some basic beliefs and received managerial wisdom will need to be challenged. And executives will need to prepare for the unexpected.

As we write this book, the future of the global economy remains uncertain. Our base assumption, as we have said, is for a sustained period of sluggish growth. But two additional scenarios remain possible: one is the risk of a "double dip"—a return to recession; the other is the prospect of a fast recovery accompanied by high demand and increased inflation.

To be credible, leaders need to acknowledge that recovery is likely to mean a long period of slow growth for the economy—

and thus slower growth for the company. They also need to consider the possibility of considerable volatility and work with scenarios that help them prepare for a sudden upswing or another downturn. To be effective, though, they need to hold out a picture of opportunity and express confidence in the ability of their company to succeed. Inwardly, they might experience tremendous uncertainty—but outwardly they will need to convey strength. This is a difficult balancing act: be too optimistic, and people will dismiss what you say; be too pessimistic, and people will lose confidence.

▣ LEADERSHIP DURING A CRISIS ▣

The demands on leaders are at their highest when times are toughest. So how do the best leaders cope? By studying past recessions—as well as some individual corporate crises—we have been able to distill a few lessons for today's leaders:

1. *Walk the floor—and be visible.* Successful leaders during the 1930s put significant emphasis on being visible to people at all levels of their companies. Thomas Watson of IBM not only engaged personally in many staff meetings to get his message across, but he also made frequent plant visits. The same holds true for Richard Deupree of Procter & Gamble. He spent significant time ensuring that employees understood the problems facing the company and the approaches that were being taken to solve them. In tough times, employees are hungry for information and leadership. In an information vacuum, they will connect the dots in the worst ways imaginable. Leaders

should hold team and one-on-one meetings to encourage people to talk about what they are feeling (and should listen with empathy).

2. *Set clear expectations.* Employees respond more positively if they have well-defined expectations. Leaders need to establish the measures of success, both for the short term and for the future. They need to provide clarity about what is most important in this environment.

3. *Mobilize the extended leadership team.* Leaders should not pilot through the difficult times on their own. They need to bring in their broader leadership group, which will provide complementary skills and multiply the personnel power and brainpower available to tackle critical issues. There is strength in numbers. Middle managers are frequently the most important leaders in times like these. They have sometimes been with the company longer than more senior leaders, and they are typically closer to the mass of employees. By respecting, trusting, and properly engaging these managers, leaders can set a positive example for how managers should treat one another and cascade the right messages and behaviors throughout the company.

4. *Keep it real.* Employees want to know that their leaders have a heart. People will rarely go the extra mile for someone who is all logic and no emotion. Leaders should be prepared to openly share what the new realities mean for them personally. This requires a willingness—even the courage—to let their guard down. Tone and delivery can and will influence how people interpret and internalize events, so it is important to pay attention to both the content and the context of messages.

5. *Drive results.* Running day-to-day business operations in a slow-growth environment will be a significant challenge. Motivating the organization when tough decisions have to be made will require a well-balanced approach. Initiatives need clearly established milestones and metrics—and unambiguous ownership. Leaders need to track progress rigorously against those metrics and milestones, intervene when necessary, and communicate any changes of direction. At the same time, leaders need to celebrate success and recognize the contributions of individual team members who have achieved results. Testimonials from customers and employees that demonstrate a company's values and strengths can be amazingly powerful and effective. Some executives think that video clips and small rewards (and awards) can be gimmicky. Perhaps—but they work.

6. *Invest in affiliation and retention.* Retaining the best talent will become an even bigger challenge in the context of slow growth and fewer available opportunities to create a satisfying career path. It is important to actively manage the attrition of lower-performing employees in order to ensure that there are career opportunities for the most talented people. Additional measures will be necessary, especially in light of demographic challenges. While leaders in the 1930s focused on securing jobs for the most skilled workers (by lowering the number of working hours per head and, when necessary, shifting high-skilled labor to lower-skilled jobs to keep them on the payroll) and also added social benefits that in part compensated for lower wages, today's leaders will have to come up with innovative approaches in the field of work-life balance and compensation.

Learning these lessons and adopting these practices will stand executives in good stead as they adjust to the new realities of corporate life and try to come to terms with the greatest set of challenges to their understanding of how business should be conducted—from the nature of globalization and the importance of politicians to the power of the shareholder and the ethics of management.

■ RETHINKING WHAT GLOBALIZATION MAY MEAN ■

Globalization has been at the top of the agenda for many executives all over the world for the past 20 years. Indisputably, the liberalization of many economies and the incredible speed of development of others—most notably China and India—contributed significantly to the buoyant global growth of the boom years. The features of globalization—rising demand and globalized production, combined with downward pressure on labor costs in the developed markets—allowed companies to reach record-high levels of profitability.

Although the new era will be marked by increased protectionism, we do not claim that the trend toward more global integration will be reversed. But it might slow down, and it will certainly change. Already, countries previously seen only as sources of cheap labor are themselves emerging as markets—with plenty of consumers. Such markets will be among the rare growth hotspots in the new era. This trend will be even more pronounced if the G-20 group of advanced economies manages to reach an agreement to rebalance global trade by increasing domestic consumption in the surplus economies. Companies will have to assess their production and go-to-market strategies in light of this development.

In addition to serving as markets, these rapidly developing economies will host a new generation of competitors—the so-called *global challengers*. Even before the Great Recession, companies from the developing economies had built a powerful international presence. In the wake of the crisis, though, these companies are emerging more powerful than before. They have the advantage of being based in comparatively fast-growing markets that have not suffered the same kind of damage as markets in the developed countries. Building on their cost advantage and their increasingly comparable technological competence, these companies will add to the competitive pressure experienced by companies of the established order.

Traditional multinational companies from the industrialized countries should not underestimate this intensified competition. And, indeed, smart companies are already taking action. Just look at General Electric. A role model from the Great Depression, GE has already started to take account of the new globalization model.

Jeff Immelt, GE's chairman and CEO, in an article he co-authored in *Harvard Business Review*, explains how GE is focusing on what he calls *reverse innovation*—a process led by GE units located in emerging markets and then disseminated to other markets.[1] This is in contrast to globalization (or "glocalization," as GE calls it), in which innovation is driven by GE units in the developed markets and then distributed worldwide with some degree of localization for specific markets.

GE argues that the "glocalization" model belongs to an era when developing countries did not offer much, either as innovators or as consumers. But, with rapid growth in countries such as China and India and slowing growth in developed nations, they see things changing fast. So GE is therefore redefining globalization and reinventing the business model to focus on the so-called BRIC countries: Brazil, Russia, India, and China. In so doing, GE is widening the market in the rapidly developing economies and preempting local challengers from creating similar products with which they could attack GE in developed markets. The offensive move is also a first line of defense for GE.

GE says that the centralized, scale-driven, product-focused structures and practices that underpinned globalization get in the way of reverse innovation because the new approach requires that resources be based and managed in the local market. It is those local teams that must decide which products to develop for their markets (because they are closest and understand them best), drawing on the company's global resources as necessary.

An example of this philosophy in action is GE's $3 billion program for health care innovation aimed at driving down costs, increasing access, and improving quality. Two radical inventions demonstrate the value of the GE approach: a $1,000 handheld electrocardiogram (ECG) device and a portable ultrasound machine that sells for around $15,000. Designed to be small and relatively cheap, these inventions are also remarkable because although they were designed for emerging markets (the ECG device for rural India and the ultrasound machine for rural China), they are now being sold in the United States.

The changing nature of globalization will require managers to rethink their entire approach to business—from research and development and product design through manufacturing and sales and marketing. Long-standing prejudices about business models should be jettisoned, and a flexible mind-set should be developed that can devise quick responses to the challenges of rapidly transforming global markets.

Globalization will not be the only tenet of modern management to be redefined. Business leaders will need to reflect on some of their other commonly held beliefs as they adjust to the new realities of business life.

■ HONING POLITICAL SKILLS ■

One of the new realities is the heightened involvement—and intervention—of governments in day-to-day business affairs. As a result, executives will have to think more carefully about how to deal with politicians, who are regaining much of the power and influence they once enjoyed in the corporate world.

Governments not only will intervene in trade and regulation, but they also will represent a big and growing part of the economy. In some industries—such as infrastructure, health care, and energy—good government relations have always been critical. But this will intensify and spread to other sectors. Executives in all industries and regions will have to put more emphasis on government relations—in order to influence not only regulation but also the scope of future stimulus programs.

■ REVISITING THE SOCIAL CONTRACT ■

It is not only politicians who are regaining the kind of influence they used to enjoy more than 20 years ago. Workers, too—and with them the unions—are poised to regain some of their lost influence.

The threat of globalizing production helped companies to reduce the power of unions and to put pressure on wages and working conditions. With this trend likely to go into reverse as politicians apply protectionist pressure and the economic equation changes, the pressure on companies to redefine the social contract between managers and workers is likely to grow.

As we have explained, some companies came up with imaginative solutions during the Great Depression concerning job protection, mobility, skills preservation, and the building of loyalty through the introduction of new benefits. And there was not just a short-term payback. IBM and GE benefited for decades afterward. For today's companies, defining new approaches to risk sharing and workforce relations could become a decisive source of competitive advantage as the world enters a period of significant demographic change—with more people poised to leave the workforce in most developed nations (through retirement) than to join it.

With a new social contract in place, it will be easier for companies to manage their way through the troubled times. A collateral benefit of making bold moves is that they give employees a rallying cry. Such moves send a strong signal to the organization and build confidence. If employees believe that management has guts, perseverance, skill, and the right plan, they will be willing to hang in there.

■ CHALLENGING THE ■
SHAREHOLDER-VALUE MANTRA

If politicians and workers are likely to grow in influence in the era of slow growth, shareholders, as we discussed in Chapter 2, are likely to undergo a lessening of their influence. This will have a direct impact on the way executives run their companies.

In particular, it will cause executives to reassess the importance of shareholder value, which has been part of the vocabulary of business for many years. In the new era, executives will need to find a better balance among shareholders, customers, and employees.

That a seismic shift is taking place became clear when Jack Welch, former chairman and CEO of GE, told the *Financial Times* that "on the face of it, shareholder value is the dumbest idea in the world."[2] This from a man who is famous for his commitment to managing for shareholder value and for his company's delivery against quarterly earnings-per-share estimates year after year.

If Welch's view becomes more prevalent, it would underline a relative loss of influence for investors—something we expect to intensify over the coming years. It would also signify a broader shift in management priorities. The tyranny of a short-term orientation toward quarterly results would give way to a medium- to long-term focus by management. In particular, executives would be better able to balance longer-term investment against shorter-term revenue-generating actions.

And, as experience shows, this is how true and lasting value is created—even for shareholders. Optimizing for the short term is not the way to create sustainable competitive advantage. So in this respect, at least, there may be a positive outcome from the Great Recession.

■ REDESIGNING COMPENSATION SYSTEMS ■

As executives adjust to the new realities—honing their political skills, redrafting the social contract between employers and employees, and taking account of stakeholders as well as share-holders—they will also need to address their own compensation, as well as that of their colleagues. In a politically combustible climate, in which there is rising unemployment and slow growth, coming up with a solution to retain and reward the best will not be easy.

Politicians, economists, and a dissatisfied public have roundly condemned bonus systems for their role in encouraging extreme risk taking—something often seen as a major cause of the financial crisis. Such a view is simplistic: the core problem of high debt levels cannot be fairly attributed to bonus schemes. Nevertheless, the level and the basis for bonus payments are likely to come under far more scrutiny in the years to come. Given that a slow-growth environment most probably will lead to lower equity returns, stock options might lose some of their appeal as well. It will be necessary to redesign compensation systems in a way that will attract and retain talent and, at the same time, reward sustained (real) strong performance. Criteria for such a redesign should include the following:

1. *An emphasis on the long term.* Investors (and politicians) want managers to focus on creating sustainable long-term value, not just beating this year's plan—especially in today's recessionary environment. Therefore, incentive compensation plans should have a bias toward the long term in the form of longer vesting periods, clawbacks, and multiyear performance targets.

2. *The reward of relative performance.* Equity-based incentive compensation such as stock options or restricted stock grants should reward executives when the company outperforms its peers, not just when it enjoys a windfall

in the stock market. Performance metrics for such compensation should be based on relative as well as absolute performance through indexing to the performance of a properly designated peer group.

3. *The measurement of performance that executives can influence directly.* Overall company performance may be an appropriate metric for the top executives of a company. But the lower one goes in the executive ranks, the less control executives have over corporate-wide outcomes, and the less relevant such outcomes become as incentives. In general, executives at the business-unit level should be evaluated according to financial and operational performance metrics that are relevant to the units they lead.

4. *A focus on value creation, not just on earnings or the profit and loss (P&L) statement.* The internal performance metrics a company uses should take into account how executives use the capital entrusted to them, not just whether they are able to meet plan targets to grow earnings per share or the P&L statement. This means that executives should be held accountable for the size and sustainability of the cash flows they generate after reinvestment as well as for the capital bets that they make.

5. *The minimizing of the asymmetries of risk.* For executives truly to act like owners, they need to experience the same kind of risks that normal investors do. In addition to allowing executives to enjoy the benefits of a potential upside, an effective incentive compensation system also must ensure that they suffer the costs of the potential downside by putting some portion of their own wealth at risk. The furor over bankers' pay quite rightly highlights

how some were able to reap the benefits from betting the bank while subsequently suffering none of the downside.

■ REDEFINING CORPORATE GOVERNANCE ■

The failure of large parts of the banking system was not simply due to rogue traders or greedy bankers. There were serious failures in risk management, control, executive oversight, and independent scrutiny. There has already been a scramble to address these issues. Regulators and politicians have been falling over themselves urging fundamental changes to fix the glaring weaknesses. Some banks have already moved to strengthen their boards, replacing worthy—but not financially proficient—nonexecutive directors with seasoned ex-bankers.

The logic is clear. The most senior overseers of the company need to be fully familiar with the technical workings of the business in order to be able to assess the risks that management is taking. And this is not just true of the nonexecutives. Senior executives need the right skills if they are to guide their businesses properly. Thus, over time, bank boards around the world must be strengthened considerably in terms of basic technical capability.

This is already happening in the United Kingdom, where steps have been taken to strengthen corporate governance. In July 2009, Sir David Walker, former chairman of Morgan Stanley International, completed his government-commissioned review of the corporate governance of financial institutions. He said that the "proposals are designed to improve professionalism and diligence of bank boards. . . . If this means that boards operate in a somewhat less collegial way than the past, that will be a small price to pay for better governance."[3] His recommendations included a 50 percent increase in the minimum time spent by nonexecutive directors on board matters and greater power to risk committees to scrutinize and, if necessary, block large transactions.

The natural extension of this approach to corporate governance beyond the financial services sector is for all boards to become much more familiar with the strategies of their enterprises—and most particularly with the risks being undertaken. Management will find it increasingly difficult to bluff their boards if the directors are well versed in the business.

Changes in the law notwithstanding, shareholders and management are already being more assertive about changing governance structures. There is no single board model; boards need to reflect the companies they are governing. In general, though, boards need to explicitly address the complex issues of their structures, the representation of necessary skills and industry knowledge, and their relationship with management. This will require the creation of a board and board committee structure that are suitable for the size and complexity of the company, as well as the introduction of an appropriate membership and processes by which decisions are made.

These trends are clearly on the minds of executives at large. In our survey, a significant majority (80 percent) expects a greater role for nonexecutive directors in holding management more accountable and in having a greater involvement in and understanding of their company's business.

◼ A DIFFERENT PERSPECTIVE ON ETHICS ◼

The financial crisis—and the resulting Great Recession—has precipitated extensive debate about ethics in the world of business. Some of this debate is a thinly veiled attack on Anglo-Saxon market-based capitalism. For such critics, the crisis was proof that free-market capitalism had failed. They saw the economic meltdown as the triumph of greed, characterized by a lack of concern about the impact of actions on others, coupled with the pursuit of personal wealth at any price. At the British Labour Party conference in the autumn of 2009, Gordon Brown, the U.K. prime minister, maintained, "What failed was the . . . idea that markets always self-correct but never self-destruct. What failed was the right-wing fundamentalism that says you just leave everything to the market."[4]

Apart from this political rhetoric, however, there is a serious underlying debate about what constitutes fair capitalist behavior—in other words, what is ethical in business. While most business leaders did, of course, adhere to strict ethical principles, there is pressure to move the borders of what is defined as good or bad behavior—and, by inference, what is good or bad ethics. The G-20 group of advanced economies may find it convenient to deflect all blame for economic mismanagement onto the unconstrained behavior of the business system, but they are also responding to public pressure to rein in the excesses. More than two-thirds of the executives we surveyed expect an increase in public scrutiny of business ethics and personal excesses. This figure was even higher for the United States and the United Kingdom.

Some of the debate has criticized the teaching at business schools, the primary recruiting ground for the finance industry. In recent years, nearly 40 percent of the graduates from top business schools have accepted positions in finance. A new oath to serve the greater good, taken voluntarily by students at Harvard Business School, met with a mixture of plaudits and cynicism. There are other, more fundamental changes taking place in curricula, with many schools agreeing on the need to emphasize linkages across markets and to place the fundamentals of business in the context of the current crisis. Also, some business schools, such as New York University's Stern School and Chicago's Booth School, expect an increase in interest in classes on economic history, particularly lessons from the Great Depression.

While it is too early to say whether these changes represent a decisive break from the recent past, what is clear is that it is unlikely to be business as usual.

■ MOBILIZING FOR GROWTH ■

There are, as we have seen, many examples of companies that have driven growth during challenging economic times. They had the courage and confidence to back their judgment about where opportunities could be exploited. Chapters 4 and 5 described the strategies. But changing the managerial mind-set will be the toughest challenge of all.

Management teams are acutely aware of the increased pressure that comes with constrained economic growth. If anything, this reinforces defensive tendencies and promotes a mind-set inclined to explain why growth is hard to achieve—rather than an attitude of actively seeking growth and a disproportionate share of the market.

This "crisis mode" reinforces what already—in normal times—are obstacles to growth: a risk-averse culture that increases in parallel with the increasing cost of failure for any individual; decision-making that slows down as managers seek extra reassurance before taking action; and leaders who become more reluctant to empower their management teams.

In the face of such uncertainty, it becomes harder to build clarity around direction and focus—and there is a bias toward the short term. As a consequence, investment programs are typically the first things to be cut back—often with insufficient thought or reprioritization.

So how can companies overcome these obstacles? Strong leadership—which serves to create a climate in which the risk of failure does not overwhelm real opportunities—obviously helps. Even when funds are short, it is still important to allow experiments and pilot programs to flourish. Keep in mind that every dollar invested has even more impact as competition scales back. One company close to bankruptcy invested in the development of a new product, in this instance a computer game, that turned out to be the source of a multibillion-dollar revenue stream.

Celebrating success and recognizing (positively) heroic failure—and rewarding both accordingly—are important. This approach can be supported by setting sensible metrics over realistic time frames. After that, the difference between success and failure lies in the execution. How well does the company understand the potential of new markets for existing products? Have the recession and the company's response to its aftermath created new compromises for customers in the way the company now undertakes its business? Does the conventional industry wisdom need challenging in light of economic developments and emerging new realities? And which elements of business economics can be fundamentally challenged in order to change the competitive rules of the game?

Such approaches do work. For example, challenging fundamental business economics has led to innovative business models such as low-cost airlines as well as online and telephone sales of insurance. And trying to offer customers the products and features they want rather than forcing them to compromise has led to developments such as the people carrier in the automobile industry. For such breakthroughs to happen, however, the managerial mind-set around growth needs to be in the right place.

■   ■   ■

The Great Recession might be over, but the global economy will remain damaged for many years to come. An era of slow growth has begun, and the new realities of business life have started to emerge. As with other major crises, the fallout from the Great Recession—and the financial meltdown that preceded it—will continue to influence the global economy and the way business is done for decades.

But, as we have explained in this book, this is not necessarily bad news for all companies. Companies and their leaders will have to get used to a time of heightened competition—but if to the victor go the spoils in any economy, this is doubly the case in a slow-growth economy. Those who take the initiative, respond decisively to the challenge, find their own way of differentiating themselves from less fleet-footed competitors, and execute their strategies with single-minded determination can still expect to grow. For those companies, the Great Recession and its new realities present a once-in-a-lifetime opportunity.

ABOUT OUR METHODOLOGY AND SOURCES

Starting with the premise that the past is an effective tool for understanding the present, we set out to learn the lessons of past economic slowdowns. The strategies highlighted in Chapters 3, 4, and 5 were selected as a result of a comprehensive historical analysis of company performance in past recessions and periods of slow economic growth. First of all, we identified companies that had outperformed their peers in times of economic difficulty; we then researched how and why they succeeded.

In order to develop our list of companies that performed relatively well in downturns, we looked at what happened during three previous periods of sustained poor economic performance: the Great Depression in the United States, the era of "stagflation" in the United States during the 1970s and 1980s, and Japan's Lost Decade of the 1990s and early 2000s. We were careful not to look at absolute performance. After all, some industries tend to fare well even during bad times (notably food, alcohol and tobacco, utilities, and health care). So we looked at relative performance, identifying companies that outperformed their competitors in terms of total shareholder return and earnings before interest and taxes (EBIT) margins.

The precise criteria for selecting outperformers varied among recessions owing to the different data available for the periods and because of the relative importance of different metrics at different times. For companies in the Great Depression, we defined outperformers as those with a total stock return performance that was better than the industry average from the 1929 peak through the 1932 trough in the market and from the 1929 peak through the 1936 peak. Our Great Depression sample totaled 90 companies—a number that accounted for around two-thirds of the 1929 capitalization of the New York Stock Exchange.

We defined outperformers from the 1970s and 1980s as those with an average EBIT margin for the period that was greater than the mean in their industry and with an average annualized total shareholder return greater than the industry median. The sample comprised companies listed on the Standard & Poor's (S&P) 1500 Composite Index.

For Japan's Lost Decade, we defined outperforming companies as those with a greater growth in market capitalization and EBIT than the industry average and an increase in market share during the period. In order to develop a broad-based comparison, we used a database of nearly 5,000 Japanese companies from the 1990s and early 2000s.

Once we had compiled the list of outperformers, we took a deeper look at what made those companies successful. We studied the markets in which these outperforming companies operated, their leadership, and the decisions they made in response to changing economic conditions. What quickly became clear from this analysis is that the actions that separated winners from losers are remarkably similar across different recessions. Regardless of the recession, successful companies have followed a combination of defensive and offensive strategies that are still applicable today.

There are some inevitable biases in our selection of companies. First, and most obviously, the successful stories—particularly those from the Great Depression—suffer from survivor bias. Other companies may well have failed despite pursuing similar courses of action—but it is the winners who get to write the histories. Second, we have looked only at publicly listed companies because of the challenges of uncovering the stories of privately held ones. And third, even for publicly traded companies, the trail back to the Great Depression often went cold. But we also learned a valuable lesson: if you look back far enough, you will find that many, if not most, modern strategies have a strong historical ancestry.

Undertaking this kind of historical research necessitated the use of a wide range of sources, and the kinds of sources varied across the different historical periods. Developing a list of outperforming companies in the Great Depression was especially challenging because aggregate company data are not publicly available as they are for later periods. Nevertheless, the Center for Research in Security Prices at the University of Chicago has managed to compile a database by poring over old newspapers—and we were able to use this.

We also relied heavily on secondary historical literature and newspaper articles to fill in some gaps in the story. Those secondary works are listed in the Bibliography.

Researching later periods proved to be much easier. In addition to publicly available data on company performance, we were able to access primary materials such as newspaper articles, industry data, and annual reports. We also turned to a range of secondary literature on the companies. Again, these sources are listed in the Bibliography.

ABOUT OUR SURVEYS

In March and September of 2009, we conducted two surveys that solicited the views of corporate executives on the business environment in their countries and industries. Some 450 executives—based in the United States, the United Kingdom, Germany, France, Italy, Spain, and Japan—responded to both surveys. The September survey respondents represented 218 companies with annual sales of between $1 billion and $4.9 billion, 166 companies with sales between $5 billion and $19.9 billion, and 60 companies with sales greater than $20 billion.

In the March survey, most executives said that their companies were struggling to adjust to deteriorating business conditions. A significant percentage of them said that they were preoccupied with their company's balance sheets and were not thinking of the broad changes taking place in their countries and industries. For example, 62 percent said that they were making their plans based on estimates of gross domestic product (GDP) growth that were higher (often significantly) than official forecasts at the time. Only 57 percent saw a threat of economic protectionism and increased government regulation. Even for those who expected shifts in government and consumer behavior, their business expectations were not consistent with those beliefs. Of the 71 percent who expected consumers to become more price sensitive in 2009, over a third were also planning to increase prices in 2009 in response to their own rising costs.

By September, it became clear that companies were taking better account of the impact of the recession. As markets picked up from March 2009 onward, the survey respondents were able to better assess the effect of the downturn on their businesses and also to better comprehend the trends in the external environment. This has led them to a better understanding of the macroeconomic and business climates.

Forecasts for GDP growth in September were more closely aligned with International Monetary Fund (IMF) estimates, and roughly 90 percent of the respondents said that they were planning for a U- or an L-shaped recession. Seventy-five percent of respondents polled in September believed that trade protectionism would increase, compared with 57 percent in March. Reflecting the public debate in their countries, this figure was higher (more than 80 percent) for trade-deficit countries such as the United States, France, Spain, and Italy, and significantly lower (roughly 65 percent) in trade-surplus countries such as Germany and Japan. A similar percentage of respondents also expected to see more policies oriented toward the rebalancing of global trade, as well as the introduction of higher levels of financial and labor protectionism.

In September, companies also predicted that governments would take a greater role in the economy for some time to come. Given the recent debate on financial sector reforms, it comes as no surprise that 80 percent of companies expected government regulation to increase. French respondents showed a clear consensus on this, with 97 percent expecting regulation to increase. Three-quarters of all companies also expected monetary and fiscal policies to remain expansionary in the near term.

A slimmer majority, however, was convinced about related opportunities for their businesses. We asked respondents whether they felt that economic stimulus measures would provide lucrative business opportunities and foster growth for their companies. Roughly 50 percent believed that this would be the case. In France, nearly 70 percent believed that the stimulus measures would create opportunities.

Companies expected to see a more competitive environment through 2010. In particular, more than 60 percent said that they were preparing for greater competition from the so-called global challengers in rapidly developing economies. This figure is even higher for the telecom and software services industries. A similar percentage also expected greater consolidation within their industries. Besides increased competition, more than 90 percent believed that increasing price sensitivity among consumers will present an additional challenge. As a result, two-thirds of companies forecasted a difficult growth environment for the next few years and lower profit levels overall.

We argued in Chapter 5 that in order to thrive in an adverse economic environment, innovation will be essential. Many of the companies we surveyed agreed. On average, 64 percent of companies expected the focus on innovation to increase in their industries; this percentage was even higher (70 percent) in the technology hardware and equipment industries. Many (60 percent) believed that this focus on innovation will lead to the emergence of entirely new business models, particularly in the retail and consumer products industries.

In planning for the future, companies anticipated changing investor behavior. More than 80 percent expected to see more conservative investment strategies. Most (roughly 80 percent) said that they expected this to result in a greater emphasis on business fundamentals, such as cash management and dividend payments.

While companies have recognized that the business environment will remain difficult through 2010, few are convinced that this will be true in the longer term. Only 30 to 40 percent of respondents believed that the changes in government, consumer, and investor behavior will persist beyond 2010. Most regard this as a shorter-term phenomenon.

We found this belief reflected in the actions companies told us they are taking. While a few have focused on longer-term defensive actions, many said they had already taken steps to expand and attack. Getting the balance right—and ensuring that defensive measures to protect the fundamentals are taken before (or while concurrently) pursuing an offensive strategy—will be especially important in a world where growth will be slow for several years to come.

NOTES

Introduction

1. Bertrand Benoit, Quentin Peel, and Chris Bryant, "Steinmeier Takes Hard Line on Regulation," *Financial Times*, February 22, 2009.

Chapter 1

1. Economic growth estimates in this paragraph and the next are from *World Economic Outlook: Sustaining the Recovery*, International Monetary Fund, October 2009, p. 2.
2. These data appear in Robert J. Shiller, *Irrational Exuberance*, Second edition, Princeton University Press, 2005, Figure 2.1; data updates are available on http://www.irrationalexuberance.com.
3. Michiyo Nakamoto and David Wighton, "Citigroup Chief Stays Bullish on Buy-outs," *Financial Times*, July 9, 2007; available at http://www.ft.com/cms/s/0/80e2987a-2e50-11dc-821c0000779 fd2ac.html.
4. Simon Kennedy and Rainer Buergin, "Soros Says 'Basically Bankrupt' Banks Restrain US," *Bloomberg*, October 5, 2009.
5. Olivier Blanchard, "Sustaining a Global Recovery," *Finance & Development*, September 2009.
6. Carmen M. Reinhart and Kenneth S. Rogoff, "The Aftermath of Financial Crises," NBER Working Paper No. 14656, January 2009; available at www.nber.org/ papers/w14656.

Chapter 2

1. Alan J. Auerbach and William G. Gale, "The Economic Crisis and the Fiscal Crisis: 2009 and Beyond," February 19, 2009; available at http://www.brookings.edu/~/media/Files/rc/papers/2009/ 0219_fiscal_future_gale/0219_fiscal_future_gale.pdf.
2. See, for example, the news release from the University of Chicago: Christina D. Romer, "The Case for Fiscal Stimulus: The Likely Effects of the American Recovery and Reinvestment Act," February

27, 2009; available at http://news.uchicago.edu/files/newsrelease_20090227.pdf.

3. Lord Mandelson's speech at the British Labour Party conference, September 28, 2009; the full text of the speech is available at http://www.guardian.co.uk/politics/2009/sep/28/lord-mandelson-speech-in-full.

4. Steve Hamm, "IBM: Outsourcing at Home," *BusinessWeek*, January 16, 2009; available at http://www.businessweek.com/technology/content/jan2009/tc20090115_770577.htm?chan=top+news_top+news+index+-+temp_technology.

5. "Europeans Fear Wave of Protectionism," Spiegel, February 11, 2009; available at http://wissen.spiegel.de/wissen/dokument/dokument.html?titel=Europeans+Fear+Wave+of+Protectionism&id=64135684&top=SPIEGEL&suchbegriff=CZECH%2C+Milosch&quellen.

6. Tony Barber, "A Shift in Gear," *Financial Times*, September 18, 2009.

7. Stacy-Marie Ishmael, "UK Consumers Adopt Depression-Era Mentality, Asda Head Says," *Financial Times*, December 12, 2008; available at http://ftalphaville.ft.com/blog/2008/12/12/50353/uk-consumers-adopt-depression-era-mentality-asda-head-says/.

8. Ulrike Malmendier and Stefan Nagel, "Depression Babies: Do Macroeconomic Experiences Affect Risk-Taking?" NBER Working Paper No. 14813, March 2009; available at www.nber.org/papers/w14813.

9. "News Release: Bank of England Reduces Bank Rate by 1.5 Percentage Points to 3%," Bank of England, November 6, 2008; available at http://www.bankofengland.co.uk/publications/news/2008/076.htm.

10. "World Economic Outlook Update: Rapidly Weakening Prospects Call for New Policy Stimulus," International Monetary Fund, November 6, 2008; available at http://www.imf.org/external/pubs/ft/weo/2008/update/03/.

11. William R. White, "Should Monetary Policy Be 'Lean or Clean'?" Federal Reserve Bank of Dallas Globalization and Monetary Policy Institute, Working Paper No. 34, August 2009, p. 14; available at http://www.dallasfed.org/institute/wpapers/2009/0034.pdf.

12. John Kenneth Galbraith: "Money: Whence It Came, Where It Went," Houghton Mifflin, 1975, p. 208.
13. Irving Fisher, "The Debt-Deflation Theory of Great Depressions," *Econometrica* (1), October 1933.
14. Ibid.
15. Ibid.

Chapter 3

1. Robert Sobel, *The Age of Giant Corporations: A Microeconomic History of American Business, 1914–1984* (Westport, CT: Greenwood Press, 1984).
2. Charles K. Hyde, *Riding the Roller Coaster: A History of Chrysler Corporation* (Detroit, MI: Wayne State University Press, 2003), p. 79.

Chapter 4

1. Michael Steen, "KLM Pilots Brought Down to Earth by Bag-Handling Duties," *Financial Times*, June 10, 2009.

Chapter 5

1. David A. Hounshell and John K. Smith, Jr., *Science and Corporate Strategy: DuPont R&D, 1902–1980* (Cambridge, UK: Cambridge University Press, 1988).
2. Jean-François Tremblay, "Shin-Etsu's Maestro," *Chemical and Engineering News* 80(40), 2002.
3. Daniel Schafer, "Siemens Chief Sees Surge from Germany," *Financial Times*, May 17, 2009.
4. John Morton Blum, *From the Morgenthau Diaries: Years of Urgency, 1938–1941* (Boston, MA: Houghton Mifflin, 1959), p. 24.
5. John F. Love, *McDonald's: Behind the Arches* (New York: Bantam Books, 1986), p. 278.
6. Yoshitaka Fukui and Tatsuo Ushijima, "Corporate Diversification, Performance, and Restructuring in the Largest Japanese Manufacturers," *Journal of the Japanese and International Economies* 21(3), 2007.
7. Joseph Schumpeter, *Capitalism, Socialism, and Democracy* (New York: Harper Perennial Modern Classics, 2008), p. 83.

Chapter 6

1. Jeffrey R. Immelt, Vijay Govindarajan, and Chris Trimble, "How GE Is Disrupting Itself," *Harvard Business Review*, September 2009.
2. Francesco Guerrera, "Welch Condemns Share Price Focus," *Financial Times*, March 12, 2009.
3. "Walker Review Proposes Fundamental Changes to Strengthen Bank Governance," press notice of *Walker Review of Corporate Governance of UK Banking Industry*, July 16, 2009; available at http://www.hm-treasury.gov.uk/ walker_review_information.htm.
4. George Parker, "Brown Takes Aim at Free Market," *Financial Times*, September 29, 2009; available at http://www.ft.com/cms/s/0/9cd0f33c-ad07-11de-9caf-00144 feabdc0.html.

BIBLIOGRAPHY

Books and Articles

Aftalion, Fred. *A History of the International Chemical Industry.* Philadelphia: University of Pennsylvania Press, 1991.

AllBusiness. "Startups Among the Ruins: How 10 Companies Launched During the Great Depression," March 23, 2009; available at www.allbusiness.com/economy-economic-indicators/economic-conditions-depression/118174551.html.

Allen, Robert C. *Speaking of Soap Operas.* Chapel Hill, NC: University of North Carolina Press, 1985.

Applegate, Edd. *Personalities and Products: A Historical Perspective on Advertising in America.* Westport, CT: Greenwood Press, 1998.

Auerbach, Alan J., and William G. Gale. "The Economic Crisis and the Fiscal Crisis: 2009 and Beyond," Brookings Institution, Washington DC, February 19, 2009; available at www.brookings.edu/~/media/Files/rc/papers/2009/0219_fiscal_future_gale/0219_fiscal_future_gale.pdf.

Bacon, John U. *America's Corner Store: Walgreens' Prescription for Success.* Hoboken, NJ: Wiley, 2004.

Bank for International Settlements. "Statistical Commentary on Provisional Locational and Consolidated International Banking Statistics at End-March 2009," July 2009; available at www.bis.org/statistics/rppb0907.pdf.

Bernstein, Michael A. *The Great Depression: Delayed Recovery and Economic Change in America, 1929–1939.* Cambridge, UK: Cambridge University Press, 1987.

Birla, Madan. *FedEx Delivers: How the World's Leading Shipping Company Keeps Innovating and Outperforming the Competition.* Hoboken, NJ: Wiley, 2005.

Bresnahan, Timothy F., and Daniel M.G. Raff. "Intra-Industry Heterogeneity and the Great Depression: The American Motor Vehicle Industry, 1929–1935," *Journal of Economic History* 51(2), 1991.

Carter, Colin B., and Jay W. Lorsch. *Back to the Drawing Board: Designing Corporate Boards for a Complex World.* Boston, MA: Harvard Business Publishing, 2004.

Chandler, Alfred D., Jr. *Scale and Scope: The Dynamics of Industrial Capitalism.* Cambridge, MA: Harvard University Press, 1994.

Chandler, Alfred D., Jr. *Shaping the Industrial Century: The Remarkable Story of the Evolution of the Modern Chemical and Pharmaceutical Industries.* Cambridge, MA: Harvard University Press, 2005.

Chandler, Alfred D., Jr. *Strategy and Structure: Chapters in the History of American Industrial Enterprise.* Cambridge, MA: MIT Press, 1990.

Collis, David J., and Nancy Donohue. "Maytag in 1984," Harvard Business School Case Study, Cambridge, MA, 1988.

Congressional Budget Office. "The Budget and Economic Outlook: An Update," Washington DC, August 2009.

Cortada, James W. *Before the Computer: IBM, NCR, Burroughs, and Remington Rand and the Industry They Created, 1865–1956.* Princeton, NJ: Princeton University Press, 1993.

Dassbach, Carl H.A. *Global Enterprises and the World Economy: Ford, General Motors, and IBM, the Emergence of the Transnational Enterprise.* New York, NY: Garland, 1989.

Datamonitor. "Industry Profile: Global Biotechnology," 2003.

Derdak, Thomas (ed.). *International Directory of Company Histories.* Chicago, IL: St. James Press, 1988.

Dutton, William S. *Du Pont: One Hundred and Forty Years.* New York, NY: Charles Scribner's Sons, 1942.

Dyer, Davis, Frederick Dalzell, and Rowena Olegario. *Rising Tide: Lessons from 165 Years of Brand Building at Procter & Gamble.* Watertown, MA: Harvard Business Press, 2004.

Editors of *Advertising Age. Procter & Gamble: The House that Ivory Built.* Lincolnwood, IL: NTC Business Books, 1988.

Eichengreen, Barry, and Kevin H. O'Rourke. "A Tale of Two Depressions," Sept. 1, 2009; available at www.voxeu.org/index.php?q=node/3421.

Engerman, Stanley L., and Robert E. Gallman (eds.). *The Cambridge Economic History of the United States, Vol. III: The Twentieth Century.* Cambridge, UK: Cambridge University Press, 2000.

European Central Bank. "Monthly Bulletin," September 2009; available at www.ecb.int/pub/pdf/mobu/mb200909en.pdf.

Farman, Irvin. *Tandy's Money Machine: How Charles Tandy Built Radio Shack into the World's Largest Electronics Chain.* Chicago, IL: The Mobium Press, 1992.

Federal Reserve Board of Governors. "The Supervisory Capital Assessment Program: Overview of Results," Washington DC, May 7, 2009.

Federal Reserve Bank of Minneapolis. "The 1929 Stock Market: Irving Fisher Was Right," Research Department Staff Report 294, December 2003.

Fisher, Irving. "The Debt-Deflation Theory of Great Depressions," *Econometrica* 1(4), 1933.

Friedman, Milton, and Anna J. Schwartz. *The Great Contraction, 1929–1933.* Princeton, NJ: Princeton University Press, 1962.

Gendron, George. "Steel Man Ken Iverson," *Inc. Magazine*, April 1986.

German Federal Ministry of Education and Research. "nano.DE Report 2009: Status Quo of Nanotechnology in Germany," Berlin, Germany, 2009.

Hall, Christopher. *Steel Phoenix: The Fall and Rise of the U.S. Steel Industry.* New York, NY: St. Martin's Press, 1997.

Heinrich, Thomas, and Bob Batchelor. *Kotex, Kleenex, Huggies: Kimberly-Clark and the Consumer Revolution in American Business.* Columbus, OH: Ohio State University Press, 2004.

Hounshell, David A., and John K. Smith, Jr. *Science and Corporate Strategy: DuPont R&D, 1902–1980.* Cambridge, UK: Cambridge University Press, 1988.

Hyde, Charles K. *Riding the Roller Coaster: A History of the Chrysler Corporation.* Detroit, MI: Wayne State University Press, 2003.

International Monetary Fund. "Global Financial Stability Report: Navigating the Financial Challenges Ahead," Washington DC, October 2009.

International Monetary Fund. "Global Financial Stability Report: Responding to the Financial Crisis and Measuring Systemic Risks," Washington DC, April 2009.

International Monetary Fund. "World Economic Outlook: Crisis and Recovery," Washington DC, April 2009.

International Monetary Fund. "World Economic Outlook: Sustaining the Recovery," Washington DC, October 2009.

Kase, Kimio, Francisco J. Sáez-Martínez, and Hernán Riquelme. *Transformational CEOs: Leadership and Management Success in Japan.* Northampton, MA: Edward Elgar Publishing, 2005.

Lebergott, Stanley. *Manpower in Economic Growth: The American Record Since 1800.* New York: McGraw-Hill, 1964.

Love, John F. *McDonald's: Behind the Arches.* New York: Bantam Books, 1995.

Malmendier, Ulrike, and Stefan Nagel. "Depression Babies: Do Macroeconomic Experiences Affect Risk-Taking?" NBER Discussion Paper No. 14813, Cambridge, MA, March 2009.

Maney, Kevin. *The Maverick and His Machine: Thomas Watson, Sr., and the Making of IBM.* Hoboken, NJ: Wiley, 2003.

Mayhew, Anne. *Narrating the Rise of Big Business in the USA: How Economists Explain Standard Oil and Wal-Mart.* New York: Routledge, 2008.

McCraw, Thomas K. *American Business 1920–2000: How It Worked.* Wheeling, IL: Harlan Davidson Inc., 2000.

McLellan, Kerry, and Allan J. Morrison. "The Diaper War: Kimberly-Clark versus Procter & Gamble," Ivey Management Series, 1991.

Miwa, Yoshiro, and J.M. Ramseyer, "Apparel Distribution: Inter-Firm Contracting and Intra-Firm Organization," Discussion Paper No. 313, John M. Olin Center for Law, Economics and Business, Harvard Law School, Cambridge, MA, February 2001.

Ndiaye, Pap A. *Nylon and Bombs: DuPont and the March of Modern America.* Balitmore: Johns Hopkins University Press, 2007.

Nicholas, Tom. "Trouble with a Bubble," Harvard Business School Case 808-067, August 2007.

Organisation for Economic Co-operation and Development (OECD). "Economic Outlook—Interim Report" Paris, March 2009.

Perman, Stacy. "Learning from the Great Depression," *BusinessWeek*, October 17, 2008.

Pitrone, Jean. *F. W. Woolworth and the American Five and Dime: A Social History.* Jefferson, NC: McFarland, 2003.

Preston, Richard. *American Steel: Hot Metal Men and the Resurrection of the Rust Belt.* Englewood Cliffs, NJ: Prentice-Hall, 1991.

Pugh, Emerson W. *Building IBM: Shaping an Industry and Its Technology*. Cambridge, MA: MIT Press, 1995.

Reinhart, Carmen M., and Kenneth S. Rogoff. "The Aftermath of Financial Crises," NBER Working Paper No. 14656, Cambridge, MA, January 2009; available at www.nber.org/papers/w14656.

Rhodes, David, and Daniel Stelter. "Seize Advantage in a Downturn," *Harvard Business Review*, February 2009.

Romer, Christina. "The Lessons of 1937." *The Economist*, June 18, 2009.

Schatz, Ronald W. *The Electrical Workers: A History of Labor at General Electric and Westinghouse, 1923–60*. Chicago: University of Illinois Press, 1987.

Schisgall, Oscar. *Eyes on Tomorrow: The Evolution of Procter & Gamble*. Chicago, IL: J.G. Ferguson Publishing, 1981.

Schumpeter, Joseph. *Business Cycles: A Theoretical, Historical, and Statistical Analysis of the Capitalist Process*. New York: McGraw-Hill, 1939.

Schumpeter, Joseph. *Capitalism, Socialism, and Democracy*. New York: Harper Perennial Modern Classics, 2008.

Shiller, Robert. *Irrational Exuberance*. Princeton, NJ: Princeton University Press, 2005.

Sobel, Robert. *The Age of Giant Corporations: A Microeconomic History of American Business, 1914–1984*. Westport, CT: Greenwood Press, 1984.

Stelter, Daniel. *Deflationäre Depression: Konsequenzen für das Management*. Berlin: Deutscher Universitäts Verlag, 1990.

Tedlow, Richard S. *New and Improved: The Story of Mass Marketing in America*. New York: Basic Books, 1990.

Tremblay, Jean-François. "Shin-Etsu's Maestro," *Chemical and Engineering News* 80(40), 2002.

Vance, Sandra S., and Roy V. Scott. *Wal-Mart: A History of Sam Walton's Retail Phenomenon*. New York: Twayne Publishers, 1994.

Verein Deutscher Ingenieure Technologiezentrum. "Nanotechnologie als wirtschaftlicher Wachstumsmarkt: Innovations- und Technikanalyse," November 2004.

Weil, Gordon L. *Sears, Roebuck, U.S.A.: The Great American Catalog Store and How It Grew*. Briarcliff Manor, NY: Stein & Day, 1977.

Weiss, H. Eugene. *Chrysler, Ford, Durant and Sloan: Founding Giants of the American Automotive Industry.* Jefferson, NC: McFarland & Company, Inc., 2003.

Wells, John R., and Nasswan S. Dossabhoy. *The Major Home Appliance Industry in 1984, Revised.* Cambridge, MA: Harvard Business School Press, 1985.

White, William. "Should Monetary Policy Be 'Lean or Clean'?" Federal Reserve Bank of Dallas Globalization and Monetary Policy Institute, Working Paper No. 34, August 2009; available at www.dallasfed.org/institute/wpapers/2009/0034.pdf.

Wigmore, Barrie A. *The Crash and Its Aftermath: A History of Securities Markets in the United States, 1929–1933.* Westport, CT: Greenwood, 1985.

Wise, George. *Willis R. Whitney, General Electric, and the Origins of U.S. Industrial Research.* New York: Columbia University Press, 1985.

World Trade Organization. "Report to the TPRB from the Director-General on the Financial and Economic Crisis and Trade-Related Developments," March 26, 2009.

World Trade Organization. "Report to the TPRB from the Director-General on the Financial and Economic Crisis and Trade-Related Developments," July 17, 2009.

Yamaguchi, Takahide, and Hiroyuki Yoshida. "Fast Retailing: An Analysis of FDI and Supply Chain Management in Fashion Retailing," Henley Business School, University of Reading, 2002.

Yanai, Tadashi. "The Secrets to Uniqlo's Overwhelming Success and Japan's Textile Industry," Brown Bag Lunch Seminar Series, Research Institute of Economy Trade and Industry, June 2001.

Other Sources

BCG ValueScience Center historical database of S&P 1,500 companies.

BCG ValueScience Center historical database of Japanese companies.

Center for Research in Security Prices, U.S. Stock & Indices Databases, April 2009 Monthly Update, University of Chicago, Booth School of Business.

IBM Archives, www-03.ibm.com/ibm/history/.

Japanese historic newspaper and magazine archives for *KABDAS Express*, *Kagaku Kogyo Nippou*, *Mainichi Economist*, *Nihon Shokuryo Shinbun*, *Nikkan Kogyo Shinbun*, *Nikkei BP*, *Nikkei Business*, *Nikkei Business Associe*, *Nikkei Business-jin Bunko*, *Nikkei FQ*, *Nikkei Ryutsu Shinbun*, *Nikkei Sangyo Shinbun*, *Nikkei Shinbun*, *Ryutsu Service Shinbun*, *Shukan Diamond*, and *Tokyo Keizai*.

LexisNexis for access to historical articles from the *Wall Street Journal*, *BusinessWeek*, and *Fortune*.

ProQuest Historical Newspapers, *New York Times*.

Roubini Global Economics (RGE) Monitor: http://www.rgemonitor.com/roubini-monitor/256382/.

Shiller, Robert. Personal Web site—historical databases of U.S. house prices and equities prices, www.irrationalexuberance.com/.

SourceOECD/Statistics.

Thomson Datastream.

U.S. Bureau of Labor Statistics.

U.S. Federal Reserve System.

BCG Publications

BCG survey. "Companies in the Downturn: Expectations, Actions and Preparedness," March 2009.

BCG survey. "Companies in the Downturn: Expectations, Actions and Preparedness," September 2009.

Evans, Philip. "The Obama Stimulus, Politics, and the Fate of the World Economy," 2009.

Freeland, Grant, Chuck Scullion, Andrew Dyer, and Rainer Strack. "Leaders Have Made The Quick Cuts—Now What?," BCG White Paper, May 2009.

Gell, Jeff, Jens Kengelbach, and Alexander Roos. "Be Daring When Others Are Fearful: Seizing M&A Opportunities While They Last," BCG Report, September 2009.

Kotzen, Jeff, Chris Neenan, Alexander Roos, and Daniel Stelter. "Winning Through Mergers in Lean Times," BCG White Paper, July 2003.

Kotzen, Jeff, Eric Olsen, and Frank Plaschke. "Valuation Advantage: How Investors Want Companies to Respond to the Downturn," BCG White Paper, April 2009.

Kronimus, André, Alexander Roos, and Daniel Stelter, "M&A: Down but Not Out: A Survey of European Companies' Mergers and Acquisition Plans for 2009," BCG White Paper, December 2008.

Olsen, Eric, Frank Plaschke, and Daniel Stelter. "Avoiding the Cash Trap: The Challenge of Value Creation When Profits Are High," BCG's 2007 Value Creators Report, September 2007.

Reeves, Martin, and Michael S. Deimler. "Thriving Under Adversity: Strategies for Growth in the Crisis and Beyond," BCG White Paper, May 2009.

Rhodes, David, Daniel Stelter et al, "Collateral Damage," BCG White Paper series (Parts 1–7), September 2008–June 2009.

Roche, Catherine, Michael J. Silverstein, Patrick Ducasse, and Natalia Charpilo. "Winning Consumers Through the Downturn: 2009 BCG Global Report on Consumer Sentiment," BCG Center for Consumer Insight, April 2009.

Sticher, Georg, and Peter Strüven. "Innovationsstandort Deutschland—quo vadis?" BCG report, December 2006.

Strack, Rainer, Jean-Michel Caye, Rudolf Thurner, and Pieter Haen. "Creating People Advantage in Times of Crisis: How to Address HR Challenges in the Recession," BCG and the European Association for People Management, March 2009.

INDEX

ABOUT THE AUTHORS

DAVID RHODES is a London-based senior partner and managing director at The Boston Consulting Group and the global leader of the firm's Financial Institutions practice. Since joining BCG in 1985, Mr. Rhodes has worked with clients all over the world, primarily on issues involving major strategy and organizational change. Mr. Rhodes has a law degree from University College, Oxford and an MBA from Harvard Business School.

DANIEL STELTER is a Berlin-based senior partner and managing director at The Boston Consulting Group and the global leader of the firm's Corporate Development practice. He is also a member of BCG's executive committee. Since joining the firm in 1990, Mr. Stelter has worked with companies around the world, directing projects with a special focus on corporate finance and strategy. Mr. Stelter holds a doctoral degree in business administration from the University of St. Gallen.